THE WAY HOME TO LOVE

A Guide to Peace in Turbulent Times

Maresha Donna Ducharme

BALBOA.
PRESS

A DIVISION OF HAY HOUSE

Scripture quotations taken from the 21st Century King James Version®, copyright © 1994. Used by permission of Deuel Enterprises, Inc., Gary, SD 57237. All rights reserved.

Balboa Press books may be ordered through booksellers or by contacting:

Balboa Press
A Division of Hay House
1663 Liberty Drive
Bloomington, IN 47403
www.balboapress.com
1 (877) 407-4847

Print information available on the last page.

ISBN: 978-1-5043-8255-7 (sc)
ISBN: 978-1-5043-8257-1 (hc)
ISBN: 978-1-5043-8256-4 (e)

Library of Congress Control Number: 2017909609

Balboa Press rev. date: 07/29/2017

CONTENTS

FOREWORD

"In your own way and at your own pace, you are walking on the path of love. That means you have inside of you a call to grow and to expand and to be a beautiful person, a good person."[1] Everyone who picks up this book has felt that call. It is a call to live in a way that is fulfilling and joyful. It is a call to live a life that is kind and giving, a life that is courageous and on point. But how do we answer that call? Is there any way to find ourselves at home in this world and not be pulled this way and that by the challenges of our own lives as well as the crises that arise everywhere around us? Maresha shows us how to bring what may feel like a place of separation into a place of unity, wholeness, and peace.

The chapters in this book are a selection of teachings distilled from discourses delivered by Maresha to students who came to be in sanctuary over the years; they came to open and receive inspiration from a master teacher. Maresha is not aligned with any particular religion or philosophy; her teachings arise from the same root that has given birth to all great spiritual teachings and traditions. Her teachings are practical and available to every one. To sit with Maresha is to feel the resonance of the divine; it is to feel your own heart fluttering and opening with the possibility of love. You will feel that resonance in the pages of this book.

The inclusion of student questions, set off by italics in the text, helps to ground Maresha's teachings. *What about this situation I have with my boss? Should I march in front of city hall, or should I stay home and pray? Will I ever move beyond the anger I feel toward my mother?* Out of the

---

[1]   Maresha, unpublished talk, May 2007.

wealth of a life forged by the fire of divine inspiration and dedicated practice, come answers and guidance to help students help themselves to find their way to liberation.

This is not a book about finding a new mate, a better job, or curing a physical problem, although these things may happen as one begins to grow in understanding and awareness. This is a book about transformation. It is about burning through the obstacles that block us from experiencing our true nature, which is love, every moment of every day. It is a book that teaches that the real discipline is life itself, and as we learn our lessons, we begin to heal and walk a balance between heaven and earth. Many of the practices that Maresha teaches: surrender, self reflection through witness consciousness, listening to guidance, and breathing meditation, are primary on the path of transformation.

Maresha often uses a word that I thrill to hear, and that word is "magic." Imagine if your life were magical, if you were able to flow with change, without fear; if your life were filled by surprises and synchronicities at every turn that fulfilled and sustained you. Imagine if you trusted love so completely, the way this universe works, that you could easily follow guidance in your actions and your words. Imagine if you could live in this world and all the while dwell in the house of love, at all times, in all places, and under all circumstances. This is the promise that beckons from these pages.

Janice Winokur, Editor
March 24, 2017

PREFACE

The kingdom of heaven is within – this is the foundational consciousness of these messages. What we are searching for is already within us. These discourses sit upon the premise that love is the all-pervading essence that is our true, inner nature. We walk on the path of love to know our nature more deeply so we may realize inner freedom by awakening our souls.

This freedom is the nature of the soul, as it is sensitive to and guided by the vibrations of the one. It all rests within our own true nature of love. We sense this. Something calls us forward. But first, each one of us must unlock and dissolve inner obstacles we unconsciously carry. We each have the ability to uncover our sacred heart and to live and walk in the beauty of love.

Even as a small child, I had memorable, spiritual learning experiences about the nature of love. My Italian grandmother soothed and healed us with an herbal drink or poultice when we were ill. She held ancient knowledge of dreams and healing. When I was four or five, one of my first friends ever was an 85-year-old, wise woman neighbor. When all the other children in the neighborhood were outside running around and playing, I preferred to spend time with Mrs. Duprat. The other children were afraid of her and called her a witch. But I was not afraid of her ancient visage; I was drawn to it. She and I would sit together and talk. Sometimes we would just sit. Later, after her death, my parents bought her house from the state. We learned that Mrs. Duprat and I shared the same birthday. She had an extensive library on astrology, esoteric spirituality, and dream work. I asked my mother to keep those books, and I still refer to some of them today. I realize now that I was given a direct, feminine spiritual lineage on which I could draw for the rest of my life. Her knowledge was deep and her love was vast.

I was fortunate to have parents who sent me to church. I was given the opportunity to become aware of the realms which existed beyond my every day experience. The golden rule, *Do unto others as you would have them do unto you*, touched some truth in my heart, even as a little girl. I had a strong desire to go to church on Sunday mornings and to be in a sacred place. My fervent hope that I would meet God there was the beginning of my inner quest.

After college, I entered the teaching profession and taught in the public school system. I was disappointed with that career and knew there was something more I had to find. My disappointment proved to be the initial phase of the first initiation I was about to enter. This initiation stripped me of all the karmic structures I had put in place. As I was disassembled, I knew I was going through a radical transformation. I did not know where it would lead, but it was changing the very course of my life. I also understood, through direct transmission, this was a life or death choice for me. If I continued in unconsciousness, I would die.

When I had this realization, I was suffering through a fever that lasted over a month. I dropped to 80 pounds and was so weak I could barely walk. In a moment of clear light, I knew I was leaving the life I had created and would now walk on the path of God's will. From that profound moment, my fever started to recede, the life force came back into my body, and I *knew* I would live. Over the next few weeks, I prepared inwardly for what I knew I was guided to do. I managed to gain five pounds, and when I was strong enough, I walked out the front door and left my life as I knew it. I took a set of cooking pots, a vegetable knife, a prayer rug, and forty-two dollars with me. I got in the car and drove down the road. I did not know where I was going. I accepted the loving guidance that was taking me. That connection to spirit has become integrated into my life and has guided my life at every turn.

It was at that point that I met Michio Kushi, internationally known teacher of Macrobiotics and spiritual living. With Michio, I discovered my true interests and began to study and practice and to fulfill my inner search. Through this training, I had some powerful, inner experiences. These new experiences helped me to let go of my programming about how to be successful and to begin to change my previous, exclusively intellectual outlook and work. *Reality is free from all notions . . . it is our duty to transcend words and concepts to be able to encounter reality (Thich Nhat Hanh).*

Michio was known for saying, "Dream a big dream for life. Develop your intuition and stay connected to the spiritual world." His words inspired me to stay open to the big dream of my life and to allow it to come forth. I wanted to know my dream and live my dream. When I was connected to spirit, I felt inspired to live my dream. For the next five years I immersed myself in Michio's teachings. I commuted to Boston to study with Michio and later lived and taught at The Kushi Institute in the Berkshires, an old monastery in the countryside. Simultaneously, I started my own practice, counseling the many people who came forward for spiritual sustenance.

Michio's teachings were a wonderful blend of taking care of both the body and the spirit. His was a true middle path. He taught that *balance* in one's body and spirit was the key to health and spiritual connection. Often he would simply say, "Balance!" From Michio, I learned about the world of duality: good – bad, right – wrong, do – don't, summer – winter, man – woman, etc. He showed us how to transcend the world of duality through achieving balance within.

One time, I brought a man with whom I had been working to see Michio. He had cancer and was seeking ways to heal himself. After more than an hour of dietary recommendations, the man confessed that at the end of the day, he still wanted to sit down and have some Scotch. He wondered if it would ruin all his other efforts for healing. I remember Michio throwing his head back and laughing, "When you drink the Scotch, sing songs and be happy!" It took me many years to understand the depth of those words. It was the "be happy" part. How could this man be happy? He had cancer.

Slowly, I came to realize the absence of conflict was the presence of love. If this man could dissolve his fear of ruining his efforts by having the Scotch, and simply enjoy his Scotch, his freedom from inner conflict could act as a healing agent. The act of self-love is the foundation of all healing. Then, no matter what the circumstances or the outcome, love is ever present. When we are balanced within, we are aware. When we are aware, love loves through everything, no matter what the circumstances and no matter what the outcome.

One day, while I was still studying and practicing with Michio, the Institute was hosting a guest teacher. People were flocking to the third floor of the old brick building where the Institute was housed, so I went to check it out. When I walked into the room, I saw a large group of people sitting in a circle. At the center of the circle was an Indian man with long, flowing hair, clothed in white. He was deeply absorbed in an altered state of consciousness. With his eyes closed, breathing deep yogic breaths, he was moving in slow motion. The movements were beautiful. The room was completely silent and everyone was collectively absorbed into this energy. There is no other way to describe it except to say, it felt peaceful and loving. It was my first experience of resonance, and I knew then that Yogi Amrit Desai, or Gurudev, as his students named him, was to be another of my spiritual teachers.

Gurudev would often say, "I did not come here to teach you. I came here to love you." Gurudev energetically introduced me to his teacher, Swami Kripalvanandji, affectionately known as Bapuji. Through Gurudev's teachings and Bapuji's transmissions, it became clear to me that my path was The Path of Love:

> *Truly, the wise proclaim that love is the only path, love is the only God, and love is the only scripture. Only love can bring unity and remove the separation between all living beings. Only love purifies the body and mind. Love is not far away; it is as close as your heart. You can find it living there without walking a single step. Love is my only path. I am, in fact, a pilgrim on the path of Love . . . .*
>
> *The major characteristic of love is the absence of conflict. When conflict is born and increases daily, true love gradually diminishes. Where conflict finds fault, love sees virtue. When love increases daily, its flower blossoms fully, spreading its sweet fragrance everywhere (Bapuji).*

Gurudev taught me how to journey within to enter the sacred inner temple. He taught me where to go when I was in need. He taught me how to source the true nature of love in my own heart.

As I absorbed his yogic teachings and lineage, I discovered my yogini Buddha nature: *Be an island unto yourself. Take refuge in yourself and not in anything else (Buddha).* This island is our own awakened nature which resides within each one of us. It is the foundation of stability and calm, and shines light on our path to help us see what to do and what not to do. Paradoxically, it connects us to that which is ourselves, as well as to that which is greater than we are, the Holy Spirit, the all pervading divine consciousness. I received my second initiation in the *kundalini shaktipat* tradition at this time. This marked the beginning of my accepting, as a young woman, the inner constructs which would change my life and give me the spiritual reserves on which I have drawn my entire life. Gurudev's love shines his lineage of light upon all who seek it.

Yet another teacher was to have a profound, lifelong influence on me. I will simply refer to this teacher as Tawa; he has no wish to be known or to teach a great many people. Tawa is a dedicated, solitary practitioner who truly lives his life in "spirit time," moving with the rhythms of guidance and inspiration. Because of his ability to penetrate facades and to see and know clearly, many are uncomfortable in his presence.

When I first met Tawa and began to study with him, I felt like running away. And run I did. I stopped seeing him without even saying good-bye. I was not ready for his power, which meant that I was not ready for my own power. I was, however, wise enough to admit deep inside myself, that I was simply afraid of him. A year or so passed, and at a time when I was desperate to progress on my path and to deepen my soul connections, I was ready to take responsibility for myself and find Tawa again. I had no idea where he was, so I started to pray to meet him again. I prayed and prayed.

One day, while I was waiting to catch a flight in the Boston TWA terminal, I turned around and there he was. I cried out in disbelief and relief that my prayers had been answered. We reunited. He agreed to see me and told me to call him when I returned from my trip. I was away for six nights, and I dreamed of him every one of those nights. The work had begun, and I knew I was blessed.

One of the most important lessons I learned from Tawa was non-attachment. He taught me how to let go of my attachments in life. Letting go of attachments opens up infinite space for the present. Expectations no longer ruled my life. As emotions arose, I learned how to witness them without becoming them. I learned how to relate to the world as it is rather than how I wanted it to be. In clear light I was more able to see through to the truth of things. The problems of this world began to evoke compassion in my heart rather than fear or anger. I no longer tried to "find" happiness. When happiness was present, I enjoyed it and then was able to let go when it dissolved. I let life reveal itself to me and dropped the need to control anything. The boundaries of my heart had expanded, and so I loved more. I felt naturally compelled to help but was not attached to the outcome. As this consciousness grew, I experienced a sense of spaciousness and freedom. This created a genuine contentment that I could never have found in temporal experiences.

With Tawa, I experienced the sacredness of all things. I learned to deeply appreciate the mystery of the great circle of life and to know my place in the circle. With Tawa, I had a crystal clear mirror to look into and see my divinity shining back at me. Thirty-five years later we remain in an abiding and deeply spiritual relationship that is perpetually imbued with wonder and beauty.

A paradox exists in the student teacher relationship. It is an important distinction because on one hand, the student must do the inner work and is responsible for his own journey. On the other hand, a teacher can also play an important role in this development.

The essential role that a spiritual teacher plays is not the same as a teacher who is giving instruction in a specific body of knowledge or skill set. A spiritual mentor's role is not so much to transmit knowledge or understanding as much as it is to inspire, within the student, the recognition of the student's own pre-existing nature. Knowledge and understanding may be imparted to the student, but by themselves, they are not the goal. The spiritual teacher points to something that is already present in the nature of the student. The teacher points to the fundamental qualities of the student's already existing nature: oneness, awareness, divinity and connection. In this way, our teachers mirror to us, our own divine nature.

ACKNOWLEDGMENTS

When I was a young woman, I had the great blessing to receive from my teacher the consciousness that, "I Am the Obstruction and I Am the Way." This golden key opened and transformed the places within me which had constrained the flow of love from my own heart. The realization that the power was within me to remove these inner obstacles, fulfilled my true longing to realize inner freedom.

My urge for realizing inner freedom was coupled with an equally intense aspiration to help others along the way. This became both my life's inner quest and my life's work. Janice Winokur, a long time friend and practitioner, graciously devoted many hours of her time to the accurate transcription of my talks and spiritual teachings which were given at the Snow Dragon Sanctuary over the course of several years. She informed me that the talks could easily be the basis for a book and of use to other seekers. She brilliantly maintained the spirit of the original talks and helped put the manuscript into its present configuration. Carol Hart also assisted in transcription and enthusiasm for this work. The many practitioners who came to the Snow Dragon Sanctuary for these conversations stimulated much of the content through their presence and their own inner quests. My husband, Neziah, ever lastingly supports me in this work and encouraged this project. His own light is ever present in these spiritual talks and messages.

These messages could not have come through without the seed consciousness and lineage of light of the holy men and women who have inspired me and from whom I have learned through direct experience. Their guiding principles taught me that love is universal whether it is expressed through the love of the Lord God, The Divine Mother, nature and the elemental world, Jesus, Buddha, the sincerely aware mind, or Krishna – all are the same. The essential natures of these holy men and women bring forth the infinite light into the hearts and minds of humanity, guiding our way through this life, on the Path of Love. They are Shamans, Yogis, Wise Women, Kabbalahists, Christians, Pagans, Philosophers and more. They are lit candles that stirred the flames of my own inner light and divinity. It has been my great privilege to receive and live in this light and share it with others. With great thanks to Mary, Giovanina, Rumilda, Michio and Aveline Kushi, Gurudev and Bapuji, Tawa, Brant Secunda, Shakmah, and Neziah. And with heartfelt thanks and acknowledgment to Janah whose own light inspired the publication of these messages.

INTRODUCTION

Over the course of thirty years, I have learned many techniques, practices, and methods for transformation and awakening, and I have applied myself to these diligently. They have all brought me to the same place, which is the place of love. I have shared these practices with countless people who have come seeking health and freedom from conflicts and problems. At the bottom of every unresolved feeling, when everything else has been stripped away, I have witnessed a deep need in all souls to love and to be loved.

Even though the discourses and talks in this book are on various topics, each one is a reflection on how to release oneself from inner conflict. As Bapuji said, *The major characteristic of love is the absence of conflict.* Therefore, each of these discourses offers a possibility for each soul to embody love and realize inner freedom. Each message speaks to the human soul trying to find its way home to love.

One of the primary challenges of this work is seeing through the illusion that circumstances *outside* of oneself are the reason for unhappiness. *If I change my job, if I change my relationship, if I have a child, and if I have more money, I will be happy.* This kind of thinking creates obstacles to inner peace because it keeps us in perpetual conflict as we try to manage and control the way our lives look.

When we begin to understand the futility of this conflict, we can then start to do the inner work of examining and making conscious the unconscious patterns of reaction in our lives—our fears, our angers, our hostility, our greed, and on and on. On the Path of Love, we learn to look within and to discipline the unconscious parts of our nature. We must do the work *inside* ourselves to free ourselves from the bondage which we created in the first place. As we do this, we are taking the first steps toward Love.

Of utmost importance, is to begin to realize the very circumstances in life that challenge us and cause pain, are not to be solved or eliminated. They are the personal doorway to liberation. Paradoxically, by paying attention to the difficulty and pain, the pain becomes the vehicle by which transformation occurs. The cure for the pain lies within the pain.

This inner work requires perseverance, kindness, respect, humility, patience, and service. When this transformational process is underway, all attachments, even the attachment to suffering, must be surrendered if the forces of love are to disassemble the ego and finally to reassemble and forge the soul into light. As one practices, a feeling of light heartedness emerges from releasing the unacknowledged energy which has been trapped by fear. When the unconscious forces are flushed out and disassembled, a transformation of the heart opens to a vast, timeless, and sacred existence.

I am the obstacle . . . Opening up to our inner obstacles is just the first half of the equation . . . *and I am the way.* The second half of the equation is holding the power *within* us to meet and transform these unconscious forces of attachment, craving, and clinging, into an awakened awareness where openness, acceptance and love can stream in.

Awakening and conscious awareness can purify the body, mind and heart. It can harness the conflicting voices that come from the body-mind split while also unifying the fragmented forces of thinking, feeling, doing, and being. This unification creates integration. It can help you to recognize and release all unconscious thoughts, emotions, actions and reactions that block your source of being. It empowers you to tune into the true self and to live in the perpetual presence of love, without standing for or against what is present. Awakening helps you to recognize that life is a perpetual, therapeutic aggravation and to use this awareness as an opening for transformation. And finally, awakening helps you to use your practice as a vehicle to intentionally activate unconscious reactions so you can then interact consciously with your fears and self-limitations and let them go.

At the heart of my teaching about awakening and conscious awareness, is the simple and profound practice of sitting meditation with breath awareness. Other methods such as breath work, sacred movement, prayer and chanting are also practiced and enhance the inner quest.

The talks and spiritual teachings in this book were given at gatherings and retreats for spiritual students and seekers at Snow Dragon Sanctuary. Each one is a message reminding us how to live a conscious life. Each one helps us to remember the true nature of love and the guiding principles of spiritual living: how to be peaceful, beautiful, more deeply connected to God, and how to sustain and nurture our faith. I am so happy to bring forth the message. I do not care how many times, or in how many ways I repeat the message. It is always a message of light. Love lives within each of our hearts. Each one of us can act as an instrument of this love, perfection, and divine will.

It is not necessary to subscribe to a formal religion. It is not necessary to believe in God. It is not necessary to change your faith. Inquire into your own real nature and believe in yourself. Loving awareness of oneself and others will reveal to you that which you already are.

There is no place to go. You are already home. There is nothing to do. You are already what you seek. Take heart and meet every obstruction within yourself that you throw in front of the flow of love. You have the power to dissolve these obstructions, clear the path, and flow in life with love.

1

THE ESSENCE OF LIFE

There is an essence that is the very energy of life. It exists in all things and at every level of existence. It is the energy of creation which gives life and from which life is made. This essence and heart of the universal intelligence is expressed in many ways. In the book of Genesis, creation is described as the "spirit of God" moving upon the face of the waters. In the East, the universal sound of om is understood to be the "divine breath" of the universe. Other expressions of this universal intelligence include chi, prana, god, goddess, great spirit, and divine life. We will refer to this essence as the Holy Spirit.

The Holy Spirit exists in all forms. It penetrates every level of existence: material, biological and spiritual. It ranges from unconscious biological functioning in our bodies, to creative and inspiring ideas and visions in our minds, to feelings of love and openness in our hearts, to the experience of connection and oneness in our spirits. It is the divine energy of matter and spirit. It animates our individual intelligence. The Holy Spirit is the great intelligence that animates all things. The Holy Spirit thus forms a bridge of connection between matter and spirit, between us and the divine.

The Holy Spirit functions within us both consciously and unconsciously. It serves us even if we do not realize it. We do not need to be conscious to realize its effects. We draw and absorb this divine energy from food, air, water, sunlight, and the earth. As we become aware of how this energy functions, we begin to experience it as a living reality and a true, inner experience. As the Holy Spirit enters our bodies, it radiates, vibrates, and charges all of our systems: lymphatic, circulatory, respiratory, excretory, digestive, endocrine, and so on. It charges and vitalizes our glands, organs, muscles, nerves, feelings and thoughts. It fuels our instincts, intellects, and spirits.

The Holy Spirit is available at all times, in all places, and under all circumstances to everyone equally. When you consciously realize the presence of the Holy Spirit, you have the key for connecting with and expressing your divine nature. You can begin to know the divine nature of your energy body by becoming sensitive and aware of its presence as it communicates with you about your body. You can begin to know the divine nature of your emotional body by becoming sensitive and aware of its ability to register intuitive promptings as it communicates with you, and you can begin to know the divine nature of your intellectual body by unifying the fragmented forces of conflicting inner thoughts. You can transcend your unconsciousness and begin a conscious relationship with the divine.

As your spiritual practices deepen, your ability to resonate with the Holy Spirit expands. This resonance softens and relaxes the places in you that are hard and unyielding; it liberates your fears and brings you into the flows of love.

When we are connected to the Holy Spirit, it acts upon us and creates a state of healing. We resonate with love as our isolation from the Holy Spirit dissolves and our fractured spirits move into unification. Simultaneously and gracefully, we are brought into perfect relationship with ourselves and the universe.

Within the ability to sustain, channel, emanate or hold one's inner light in absolute consciousness, exists an implicit, radical faith that allows one to risk everything.

This risk cannot be calculated by degrees of riskiness. One cannot say, "I'll risk just so much now, and maybe a little bit more next time."

Everything means everything; it is literally all or nothing.

CHAPTER

2

TRUSTING LOVE

The Golden Center

The quest of the spiritual pilgrim is endless. The quest is a longing that draws one forth into the unknown, into the mystery. We cannot grasp or clearly define what it is we are being drawn toward. We only know we are going from what is known into the unknown. Many try to create controllable boundaries within which to live. Habits and patterns which are passed down become comfortable points of reference for life. Within those boundaries, we have an illusion of safety and comfort.

The seeker steps outside the box and expands the boundaries of what is comfortable and safe. All attempts to understand, know, and control are released. The seeker is thereby liberated from what is already known and returned to the pure nature of innocence. This opens the possibility for the mystery to be revealed, much like a surprise.

Being in this state of innocence is to trust love. In trusting love, we shed the masks, performances, and controls. We expose the uncovered face, and we live from our essential nature and invite wonder into our lives. This is the spiritual journey. The spiritual nature refuses certainty, dogma, and social programs. Trusting love is a radical severance from preferences, addictions, and obsessions. It is a persevering willingness to enter and re-enter the unknown. It is a commitment to listening to the voice of one's soul anew each day.

What are we trusting when we trust love? What is this love? This love is a willingness to open ourselves to a higher will; it is an absolute acceptance that we are not the initiator. We give up the ego and walk to the water so we may immerse ourselves in the stream of consciousness, and love, and merge with the infinite mystery.

We hold this inner posture in every situation we meet. Outwardly, the actions of our lives' look like everybody else's. Inwardly, we let life be revealed. We rise to every occasion with acceptance and grace, knowing that the divine is working through us. We live an ordinary life in an extraordinary way. Even the simplest act is performed differently by one who is free.

Trusting love is round, intuitive, receptive, and flowing. It moves without obstruction, open to the unknown asking to be shown, and being endlessly surprised at each revelation. It is simple, clear and honest. Trusting love means that each day you begin anew, exactly where you are. There is nothing special to do, there are no requirements to fulfill, nor do you have to go to any special place. The inner posture of acceptance and trust creates an ability to meet life exactly as it is.

Liberation lies within each one of us. When you trust love, you can observe and respond both to the mundane rhythms of life as well as to the extraordinary mystery of the eternal quest.

Trusting love is symbolized by the beauty of the perpetually blooming rose. Open to receive the light, it maintains a state of perfect openness. . . . *turn your gaze to the beautiful garden which blossoms under the radiance of light. There is the Rose in which the Divine word became flesh: here are the roses whose perfume guides you in the right ways.*[2*] There is a golden center in each rose. The golden center reminds us to still the mind, breathe in beauty, accept everything, and to trust the love in which we have immersed ourselves. The golden center calls us into the mystery.

---

2   *The Divine Comedy, Paradiso, 23, 71-75,* Dante Alighieri.

Expanding the Boundaries of Love

Expanding the boundaries of your consciousness is the same as expanding the boundaries of love. When you begin to trust love, you will see through the eyes of spirit that you are self-creating, and what is real for you is created by you. If you are willing to release that which no longer serves you, then you can begin to extend the boundaries of your love.

Drop the tape or the pattern that says, *I'm not good enough for love,* or *That's too risky. I will get hurt. I will get used. I will not have enough. I will be rejected. I will lose control. It's not going to work out well,* or *It's going to end badly.*

How do we get through these places? We get rejected, we get used, and we lose control. We are found out to be the culprits we are. Trust means that you have to be willing to be exposed for who you really are and to take a risk and get nothing in return. You must be willing to face lack and rejection along with the reality that things never do work out the way you planned anyway.

What happens when you do that? You find freedom when you release your attachment to your fear of things not working out, of being used, of not having enough, or of being rejected. Expose yourself, show everything that is there, let it all be seen, and then there is nothing to hide. If you do not risk everything, you will never be able to expand the boundaries of love.

You have to be willing to be a fool for love. You have to be willing to change your position because your position is your ego. You have to be willing to be seen and be used. What is it to be used? It is to give with no expectation of anything in return. The problem is selfishness, egocentricity and self-absorption. You are so busy trying to protect yourself or perpetrating harm upon others to satisfy your needs that you drain your life force and end up in pain instead of in love. All of your life force is lost in positioning yourself against something that you created in the first place. Then you are exhausted, rejected, tired, it did not work out, and you were right.

How could you be anything but right? You created the whole scene, and every encounter you create will bring the same result over and over again. You will be self-justified, and you will win the scene every time because you created it. You will be abandoned and rejected because you believe it to be true. If you believe it to be so, how could it be other than what you created?

You have convinced yourself in every scene, every relationship and every situation, that you are right. You will say, *See, I was right to hold on because I'm not getting anything out of this anyway. I've only been hurt.* Your self-absorption brings you to a dead end that you keep circling and projecting onto everyone and everything.

Stop the projection and release the tape. Put in a new tape that says, *I trust love.* Be willing to take a risk. Do you know what will happen when you take a risk? You will face rejection and abandonment, and you will also face getting used. But none of this can touch you if your heart stays open and in love, and if your heart trusts love. You will see those things for what they are, which is fear. It will not destroy you.

Instead, you will grow compassion and you will no longer take everything personally. You will understand that someone is playing a role for you so you can extend the boundaries of your love. Or, you will see that you can have compassion for those who are limited in their capacity to open their own hearts, and you will not judge them when they make mistakes.

When you fix your eyes on the divine, you will be fed from the infinite fount. There is always enough, it always works out, you get used, and you are blessed because of it. You accept everything. Rejection no longer exists, and all of the imperfections you have been hiding from for so long, can be accepted and healed. Spirit is benign, loving, mysterious and wonderful. You can trust love, and you can trust your heart to know love. Be willing to let your heart break. Be willing to give something and get nothing in return. It may not look like you are getting anything in return in a specific and deliberate way, but everything you give comes back tenfold. The infinite energy of the universe can cycle back to you in your fearlessness. You will find out that love has nothing to do with attachment, jealously, control or ownership, and your heart will be in love at all times.

We find liberation only by taking a risk, by taking whatever it is at the core and flipping it over. If you are greedy, then give. If you are fearful of rejection, stop rejecting and accept. If you are afraid of exposure, expose. Release your fear and be that which you want.

> *How do I go after what is in my heart and not be attached?*

When the hurt and rejection come, let them come. Let them wash through you like a wave. Feel everything completely and then let the wave recede.

> *But can't I shut out the pain so that I do not have to be hurt?*

That hurts even more because you not only shut out the possibility for being hurt, but you also shut out the possibility for love. If you take a risk and trust love, even if it does not turn out the way you wanted, you have still given yourself the opportunity to love. Drop all your concepts around how you think it should turn out, and then there is nothing to be hurt.

> *When other people do not respect or acknowledge what I have to offer, it does not feel good.*

Other people do not have to respect or acknowledge what you have to offer. *You* have to respect what you have to offer. You have to acknowledge yourself. Clear out the space, go inside of yourself, and learn how to give yourself what you need with Spirit. Other people are just bringing up your feelings of lack of self-worth; they cannot give to you what you cannot give to yourself.

> *Why do I feel so much emotion in those situations?*

Just feel the emotion. Let go of feeling that you should get something, and just be the pure emotion. When you do not ask why, you are trusting love. The emotion will come in like a wave and wash out like a wave. Stand in your core. Learn to let those places wash in and wash out. When you do that, you will stand in love. You will not put up any barriers. As soon as you do not like something, the edges of your ego are blocking love.

Feel your pain and disappointment, but let it be pure so that it burns in your tears, and then it is dissolved. Even though you feel rejected, go forth anyway because you trust love. When you know it is not personal, you do not have to isolate yourself from people anymore. When your heart stays open, you will have more capacity to accept and love people exactly as they are. Release your judgments and trust love.

Spirit has its way with us, and you either surrender to it or you do not. When Spirit puts you on hold, stop. When you are pushed forward, go forward. When something is taken away, let it go. When something is given, receive it.

Trusting love means dropping your position; it means not fighting. Surrender is an active choice. It does not just happen; we have to choose it in the moment it is presented. Surrender means there is no separation, isolation, or positioning. It is accepting what is; it is staying round and whole. It is releasing judgment and trusting love. If you fight against the ego, it will gain strength. Trust the place in your heart that tells you that this is a loving and benign universe that is abundant and supportive, and then take all of the risks to prove it to yourself. Do that by trusting love.

Love Asks You to Expand Again

You use the word risk all the time. That used to throw me because I always thought of something drastic. Now I know that taking a risk might mean speaking the truth or saying "No." Taking a risk doesn't have to mean leaving my marriage to go to India to find my guru.

That is right. Your guidance might not give you permission to do or say something, and your mind might wrestle with "What will they

9

think?" or "I don't want to offend anybody." The risk is to follow the guidance, to trust love. There is a risk in it because you are used to doing things a certain way according to your pattern, and you do not want to offend anybody.

But there are also times when our lives feel especially risky, like when we go through a divorce or lose a job. "Will I be safe, will I be taken care of? Will I be loved?"

Years ago I had a relationship that lasted for ten years. One day my partner drove out of the driveway and never came back. He left me with all the debt, mortgages and loans, none of which I had when I met him. There was everything in the world for me to fight against. I realized I was either going to become bitter and end up in a court battle over the next two or three years, or I was going to let it go and let myself be taken care of by the universe and be loved. I chose expanding my boundaries to receive more love. So I said, *I'm not going to fight. I'll take it all.*

I did not fight, and I took it all. I took on the mortgage and all the debt by myself. I did all the things that God gave me to do: running the Sanctuary, doing healing work, conducting yoga teacher trainings, and all of the other things I was given to do. Not only did I take care of everything that needed to be taken care of financially, but my life flowed and was supported in a beautiful new sequence which I could never have imagined. Those were the temple years. I was living from temple to temple, with Shakmah at The New Seed Sanctuary and with Gurudev, first in Pennsylvania and then in Florida. That was my life, and it was absolutely, extraordinarily beautiful.

The thing about love is that it asks you to expand all the time. And when you expand, you have to break through the wall within you that wants to keep you in one place. The wall says, this is your comfort zone, this is what you feel good believing, these are the people you like to be with, and these are the things you like doing. These things over here? No.

Love does not work that way. When you expand, you give up your comfort for a while. And once you expand in one place, as soon as you have expanded into that, love asks you to expand again. And so, you become very, very big.

The amount of light your energy body can sustain is directly proportional to your mindful awareness of the breath, as you inhale and exhale in pranayama. The light is the vehicle for transformation. The light's intelligence inherently works on your behalf. All you have to do is consciously breathe.

CHAPTER

3

THE TERRITORY WITHIN

Instilling the Practice of Meditation

The territory on the inner planes is vast. When you go within, you are able to see things from a completely different perspective. This territory allows you to see there is a part of you that is not structured, not habitual, and not predictable. It is infinite, intuitive, and filled with light.

When our attention is consumed by the material world day in and day out, we become creatures of habit. We react in the same way over and over again. But you have been blessed with the privilege of consciousness so you can change your habitual nature. You can learn how to respond instead of react in habitual and predictable ways.

You may already know yourself well enough to spot your reactions. You may know that if someone says something or does something in a certain way, it presses a button in you. You may also see that the way you react to life, and the decisions you make everyday, are based on the habits you have created for your comfort.

If you think in your mediation, "Well, I feel like I'm just sitting here, and my back is tight, and I have so many thoughts," that is fine. That is still meditation. Do not judge your experience or feel as if you are not making progress. The fact that you are willing to sit in one place for a period of time and not react to the world in the same way, is phenomenal. That practice is everything. Do not judge what is happening as good or bad when you sit down. Do not judge yourself if you fall asleep and your head bobs, and then you wake up and say, "Oh my God, I'm supposed to be meditating." Do not judge yourself if you start to worry about your taxes. The important piece is that you are willing to sit with yourself and not do anything but sit and breathe. In that practice you are learning how not to react to the same old things in the same ways. Even though all that stuff is still there, you are just watching, and you are watching from the witness consciousness, noticing thoughts, emotions, and anything else that arises. The witness is you watching your self; it is you in self-reflection.

The witness has the ability to watch from a neutral place and notice what is, without doing anything about it. It is not discussing or analyzing your situation; it is not doing anything but watching and witnessing. That part of who you are changes everything. You will get used to working with the witness as you sit in meditation practice. The witness will become very stable and will follow you wherever you go, because it is you.

Then one day you will be having a conversation with someone, and that person will say something that causes a reaction. The witness will allow you to see that, but the witness will also allow you to simply breathe, and by breathing, you will stay neutral. When you engage the breath, you are more likely to respond rather than react in a habitual way. Eventually most of what you do in reaction will fall away. You will be much more integrated and grounded, and much less reactive in relationships of all kinds. You will be more peaceful because you will be in a harmonious place.

Once you have instilled this inner practice, it grows stronger and stays with you wherever you go. No one needs to know anything about your inner process of breathing and witnessing.

We are so limited in the ways we think about ourselves. We identify with our bodies, our simple experiences, and whatever is concrete in front of us, but there is so much more than that. When you consciously

13

breathe, those areas become imbued with light. Every time you inhale, there is light held within the breath, and you can grow your light body so that it is not flickering on and off all the time, but really sustaining the light at all times, in all places, and under all circumstances.

The amount of light that you are able to sustain, directly affects your ability to manifest whatever the will of the Divine is bringing to you. The light holds the inspiration and the guidance that comes to you and makes it possible for you to be grounded in that, no matter what else is happening. All sorts of challenges get activated by the light, but the part of you that sits and breathes in stillness remains steady within you. That part knows what the guidance is, and sustains the light and enables manifestation to come into being.

The Focus in Meditation

Do you recommend a specific focal point in meditation,
such as the tip of the nostrils?

The focal point is always the breath, listening to the sound of the breath and feeling the sensation of the breath in the body. A good place to begin your meditation is with the Golden Circle[3] breath. This breath is drawn in through the back of the throat, and if it is done correctly, you will hear a sound, almost like a tire being inflated. The Golden Circle breath slows the breath down and starts to bring us into a meditative state. As you inhale, pull the breath all the way down into the lower belly, upper belly, chest, and then exhale completely. In the beginning this may feel mechanical, but later on, you will use the Golden Circle breath for focus and attunement, and then eventually the breath starts to breathe itself. The breath will become very relaxed. Just three or four of these breaths can bring you into a state of deep relaxation. Later you may not hear so much of the sound, but you will use the breath to re-focus from time to time.

The mind is naturally going to wander. Notice whatever thoughts

---

3   See Golden Circle Breath, Appendix.

and feelings arise. Simply breathe and notice them, letting them come in and go out. As you close your eyes, let your awareness coalesce in the third eye, the *ajna chakra*, in between the eyebrows. Focus all your awareness there, because it is the chakra of integration. The third eye integrates your higher self and your soul. Later you will be able to meditate very quickly, entering by focusing with the breath and then just abiding in the third eye, staying in the third eye awareness.

It Arises, It Is, It Dissolves.

What's the difference between watching thoughts come and go, and handling strong emotions that want to keep us in their grip?

Before you feel an emotion, you have a thought. The thought might say, "I'm afraid of this," or "This really makes me mad!" The thought happens first in the mental body, but most of the time we do not see that because the emotional body reacts to the thought, and we get caught there. Maybe our feelings were hurt, and we cannot let it go because it is so strong. But when that happens, we stay neutral by using the witness consciousness. We are watching that emotion, just as we were watching the thought that came in and passed by.

The emotion is not a thought that passes through the mind like a cloud. The emotion is felt in the body. You might feel tightness in the chest, or you might feel your heart beating a little faster. When the feeling has a significant charge and is not letting you go, let yourself feel it completely. *It arises, it is . . . .* Do not suppress any of the charge the emotion is carrying with it. As you sit in meditation, stay neutral, even though the emotion may be raging within. You are not fighting, you are not unloading on someone else, and you are not crying on somebody's shoulder; you are sitting with yourself and with the breath, and feeling the energy even as you watch it. *It arises, it is . . . .* What you do with that emotional intensity is, consciously breathe in and breathe out. You *have* to keep breathing because what usually happens in an emotional reaction is you stop breathing, and as soon as you stop breathing, the energy gets stuck.

What happens to that energy? You might get distracted because you have to run an errand or bring the kids to soccer. But after soccer, you go right back to it. The next day comes, and it is still with you. People can get stuck in a place for a long time, but that is because they are not breathing. If you continue being neutral and if you continue breathing, the breath actually starts to neutralize the charge by dissolving it. *It arises, it is, it dissolves.*

If the emotion is highly charged, you may not be able to neutralize it in one meditation session. In a beginning practice, it might take days. But, you will not hold on to this all your life, which is what most people do: same reaction to life, over and over again. But that can change.

We feel justified in our habitual reactions. We feel we are right, and we justify our position by building a case and believing it, and then we think it is real. The truth is, it does not matter in the territory I am telling you is so vast. These reactions are crusty, harmful, and afraid, and it is part of being a human being. When you release your opinion and your position, and you say to yourself, "Maybe I don't know what I'm talking about, maybe I'm not right, what do I know?" the energy loses its charge.

On a certain level, your preferences do not matter. Life never goes the way you plan it anyway, right? There is a divine plan and there is life, and the days will go differently from what you plan. Things will never be exactly the way you want them to be. You always have the ability to expand into the light, to flow harmoniously through all that, and be happy. *May you never be the least little bit unhappy, ever.* That is Bapuji's prayer for all of us. As the cliché says, "Don't sweat the small stuff."

Or even the big stuff.

We make the stuff big. The size of the challenge is increased by our habitual response. Who would we be if we had no opinion, no position, and no preference? What is left? That is what you have to find out. Who will you be when you peel back all the layers of who you think

16

you are? That is where you will find the abiding harmony, peace, and integration, but you are afraid to let go in the process of getting there because if you let go, you lose control. This is where you abdicate the small self and allow the soul to be in the driver's seat.

Take the practice of witness consciousness with you. Those of you who know it, continue to deepen with it. For those of you to whom it is new, take a portion of your meditation just to observe and see what is there, and continue to visit that vast, infinite territory of light. You can only get there by closing your two eyes and going within.

The Void Holds All the Answers

You sometimes speak of going into the void; is there any difference between that and meditation?

There is no difference between going into the void and going into silent meditation. Everybody is afraid to go into the stillness, into the void. You are afraid to face the vastness where it is just between you and God.

Nobody wants to be still. Everybody wants to have adventures and be filled with sensation. Everybody wants to interact socially and do anything but be quiet and face the void. The void holds all the answers, but in order to get them you have to become nothing. You have to be willing to face parts of yourself that want to stay unconscious because we meet those parts along the way as we journey into the void, as we journey into the resonance of the still point. When we face the void, all those unconscious parts get transformed into a beautiful, peaceful place that feeds the whole as nothing else can.

So when you're in the void, and you feel what you're feeling, there's nothing to do. You just watch and see how your life unfolds?

There is nothing to do, there is no place to go. You move according to how you are inspired to move. You observe your inspiration, you observe your promptings. What you love will speak to your heart, and your *dharma* will speak to your heart. Everything will speak, but people do not listen. They listen to everything else outside of themselves, and they listen to their ego, the part of themselves that is not connected to the resonance of the still point, the part that wants to seek the sensation, the adventure, and the longed for fulfillment that will never come.

What is it that fills us when we go into the void? We are filled with God. This is how we make contact. We are able to directly experience union and communion with the resonance of God. It is right here, within each one of us. But we act as if it is so hard to get to. That is why spiritual retreat is so important. For the most part, we do not take time to allow ourselves to journey within in a deep, sustaining way. The retreat makes it possible to go in and be there.

The Light of the Absolute

The Light of the Absolute is the point from which our higher consciousness observes the emotional life of the self. We see ourselves from a neutral, detached position, without judgment, analysis, embarrassment, doubt, or fear. We regard ourselves without an impulse to alter our circumstances or ourselves. From this place, we can experience the darkest night of feeling as we watch ourselves calmly and with clarity. The detachment of the Light of the Absolute is not one of disassociation from feeling, but rather the courage to enter into feeling with open eyes. From here we recognize our feeling without any need to think it into self-justification, self-pity, or self-criticism. Our worst feelings then remain disentangled from our identity. Our thoughts do not cement our insecurity, fear, anger, or sadness into a sense of who we are.

We enter this light by the action of the breath, and we can enter it at any time. At work, in relationships, or in a traffic jam, you can breathe yourself into the light of the absolute. By consciously breathing the slow, steady, and continuous breath, you can quickly move from unconsciousness to higher consciousness. From this place, you will know yourself better and refine who you are. You will watch your feelings pass through you, you will see their path, and you will observe their characteristics and consequences. You will see how they return again and again in a relentless pattern. You will learn to recognize them quickly, and then you will let them go. When you bring yourself to the light of the absolute frequently, you create your own healing.

This is what love is, the acceptance of the self. The heart knows the spirit and it expands within the light of higher consciousness. The light of the absolute exists in the dialogue between the heart and the third eye. The heart opens to accept the self, and one's higher consciousness sheds light upon the heart.

It is time to realize the nature of the gifts bestowed to you as a soul by God. Held within each trial and test in life is a golden center. Each soul is tried and tested. If the soul passes the test-the initiation-a deeper understanding of the real nature of love is revealed.

If you hold fast in enduring faith when being tried and tested and when everything looks most bleak, the light in the golden center bursts forth, purifying everything within and without. This cycle repeats itself over and over again, giving each soul the perpetual blessing of transformation and union with light.

CHAPTER

4

FINDING PEACE IN TURBULENT TIMES

Creating Peace

When confusion, chaos, and disruption are all around, dwell in the eye of the storm. The center is even and calm. The forces of conflict and separation are at work in the world, and we are suffering from the illusion that there is self and other, or self and opponent.

The self in relationship to the soul is the entry point to healing. On the path of love, we begin with ourselves. The first step is to bring the body, emotions, and thoughts into balance through spiritual practice. These practices help us to ground ourselves and realize balance and harmony whether we are in the midst of calm or chaos. The second step is to extend that harmony to our primary relationships with family, relatives, and friends. The third step is to extend the harmony even further into community, society and the greater collective. This creates an anchoring of wholeness and harmony. Transformation starts with each individual and ripples out from the center to reach the collective. If the realization of harmony, balance, and peace is possible for one, it is possible for all. We are all one heart.

The spiritual practices remain the same whether we are in the midst of calm or chaos. The challenge feels greater, of course, when chaos reigns. The center can be maintained at all times and in all circumstances through the regular practice of meditation, resonance movement, and prayer, as well as through the conscious relationship with one's own feelings. The feeling center is the entry point to inner knowing, or intuition. Intuition is the one-on-one relationship between you and God. These accelerated times demand that we dwell in the center of our intuitive awareness. Only our intuition can guide us moment by moment.

The energies we are living with now give us the opportunity to exercise our inner awareness to help ground us in a simple and clear way. If we choose not to develop this inner awareness, we will split and fragment into the chaos. Intuitive awareness is *not* acquired from some place outside of oneself; it is within each and every one of us, and it can be developed. It is fully present in your subtle body or feeling center. It is you, connecting with God.

We access the feeling center by slowing down, breathing deeply, and becoming still within. In the stillness lies everything we need. It is already there. Let go of the busy mind and distracting thoughts. In that open space, is simple being. Watch and observe, and be attentive to what is happening within you and around you. Empty your mind and become a silent observer. This is a meditative practice you can develop and learn. You can shift into this awareness either with your eyes closed in a quiet setting, or you can practice it as you witness the violence and fear swirling around us.

The emptiness creates space. That space creates the possibility for the unknown to be made known. To see anything new, the mind must let go of the past which repeats itself in today's agenda. Release your agenda and be fearless enough to let go of personal obsessions, addictions, attachments, and preferences. Touch the unknown. The effortless stream of life is flowing within you.

The emptiness holds everything you need. From this space, your life opens and is revealed to you. In this infinite space, lies the possibility to reach out beyond the self to others. Our essential nature is to give. When we are not preoccupied with self, there is so much you can give.

In this time of unrest, we are challenged to learn how to move out of separation and darkness. We can grow and develop a direct connection to the sweetness of life and to the source of light. Connect with this source. Breathe it in deeply and share its radiance with others. When you hold no opinion and no position, all can be revealed. In this center of space and light you become simple and stable, and this stabilizes everything else.

The practice of meditation, prayer, and self-reflection can bring us into direct connection with the soul and allow us to feel the sweetness of life and to tread the path of love. The possibility for creating peace must begin within each one of us as we become peaceful within ourselves. We are part of the whole. Our task is to heal separation, isolation, and defense of us as opposed to them within ourselves first; then we can bring that conscious awareness to all sentient beings in the world. Becoming whole in oneself and in one's consciousness is the same as becoming whole in one's family, community, society and the greater collective of the world we live in.

The soul is the point of power and the power is now, in this moment. Surrender to the natural longing within your heart to give and to love; surrender to the love that knows no separation. In this state of love, all division and separation cease.

Staying on Point

The kingdom of heaven is within us and it is reflected from the outer dimensions as in a mirror to us. In Buddhism, this kingdom within is called Shambhala, and it is said to pulsate infinite possibilities of universal truth. The basic goodness that is at the foundation of humanness resides there. In this place, we have never lost or forgotten our divinity. We have never forgotten that we are the way. But at some point, we forgot our divine birth, and that is what separated us. We always have the possibility to look into this mirror of light and infinite love if we choose.

When you speak of the mirror, I'm lost there.

When I look at the sun, the sun is my golden light. When I look at the moon, the moon is my golden light. When I look at the blue sky, I am transported into infinity. When I feel and look at the beauty of the earth, it is all a mirror for me, and I take the mirror. It is all my beauty, my enlightenment, my golden light. I drink it in, and I participate and accept the love that is everywhere for me, and for everyone.

That is the cycle of grace, and in that way, I do not forget my divine, enlightened birth this moment, now and only now.

But if you did not remember that . . .

Then it would be nothing because we are never satisfied with this now. We always want another now. As you are developing, and you see yourself doing this, call upon God and all the beautiful spirits who surround you to quickly re-establish your view so that you see goodness and beauty. *Oh, wait a minute, I'm alive right now, thank you. I have everything right now, thank you.* The divine nectar is everywhere in this life if you stay on point and sustain your view at all times, in all places, and under all circumstances.

Staying on point is staying in the present moment of now. It is not trying to be anywhere else but where you are; it is not wanting anything other than what you are given. It is being grateful, peaceful, and generous, no matter what. Good, bad, rich, poor, indifferent—the outer circumstances never take us off point.

These times, which are filled with one crisis after another, are reaching an apex. But it is a universal law that everything rises and everything falls. As warriors on the path, we learn how to ride those waves and do it while everything is groundless. Do not try to stabilize anything because you cannot do it. What is stable is your inner ability to flex and move from moment to moment, so you meet each moment with awareness. And in each moment, everything is given. We have a perpetual feast before us, and it has nothing to do with being entertained or with anything that is outer. It has to do with our inner ability to attract the mirror of light.

So as we attract that mirror of light, why do we still look around and see violence and the perpetration of atrocity everywhere?

It is part of this dimension. As you face yourself on this path, and you see people in this world who are doing what you do not like, realize they are a mirror for the aspects of your own self that you do not want to face, feel, or sit with. You want to do anything but meditate and sit with those aspects of self.

I do see seeds of violence in myself from time to time, and I see negativity as well, but it's the extremity of the violence and conflict I see everywhere that shocks me. Why am I still magnetizing that?

You see these things because we live in this dimension, in the world of opposites. We came in from the one vibration, whether you call it heaven, whether you call it God or Shambhala or whatever you want to call it, the one vibration of infinite universal energy. It splits and bifurcates in this dimension and creates the poles of good and bad, right and wrong, night and day, and do and don't. All of it exists here.

The task is not whether you see these things in the world or people who create atrocities, it is whether you can see them and maintain your own basic goodness. If you focus on their injustice or atrocity, you vibrate with their injustice and atrocity. If you witness their injustice and atrocity and stay neutral, you will maintain your own basic goodness and light, and *that* will help stabilize the other. But if you become judgmental and harsh, then the same energy cycles back and forth, maybe not to the same degree, but certainly on the same frequency.

How did that place of basic goodness get so covered up in those who perpetrate such violence and harm? I want to do something about it!

You can do something about it. You can learn how to keep yourself flexible and fluid in the midst of it all. Meeting yourself in meditation and spiritual practice can change the world. Do not worry about the demons in the world; worry about the demons that drag you around every day, the ones that keep you from being liberated and free. You *can* do something about it.

We humans have been fighting and overpowering each other since the beginning of time. This is not new. The group mind wants to polarize on opposite ends of the spectrum, and when we do that, we create an equal energy for the fight. The kind of warrior you want to be is a spiritual warrior. That is where you want to direct your attention. Be vigilant over your own obscurations of light.

The mirrors we see in the world are aspects of self, but where we address the heart of the mirror we are seeing, is through our own heart of self-reflection. It is easy to see other people and judge them. It is much harder to see ourselves in the mirror and to self-reflect.

We know that we are flawed, but we do not use the flaws to hurt ourselves. We see them from the light of our basic goodness so that we never hurt ourselves. When we look into the mirror, we remember that basic goodness is the foundation of our humanness, and the flaws we see are but our own obscurations of the infinite love that pulsates everywhere. With a warrior's eye, we can self-reflect and see our shortcomings and not be put off by them; in fact, it gives us the key to where we are going and what we are doing here.

The Dark Aspects of Self

> *So you're saying that when I look at this reflection or this infinite fount of love that pulsates all around me, and I continue to see dark places, those places are my own obscurations that are hiding the light. Those places are images and mirrors of my shadow self.*

Yes, and as you look out, that which is reflected back to you is influenced by the lens you choose. Do you choose the lens of the emotional body? Do you choose the lens of the mental body? Do you choose the lens of and higher consciousness? As souls, we get to choose, and as souls we get to exercise our choice. The soul sets out to dissolve these obscurations one at a time. Whether you are on a conscious path or an unconscious path does not really matter. Just being alive and learning the lessons of being a human being and interacting with other human beings, teaches us. Sometimes it hurts, sometimes it is hard, and sometimes it is dark. And sometimes the door opens and the light floods in, and there is union and harmony. It is all part of the process of the soul, and the soul knows its own nature, and its own nature is the nature of God consciousness. It is light, it is love, and it is all of the higher things that open our hearts and bring us peace.

All human beings have seen dark aspects of self, and all human beings have realized lightness of being through humor, communion, and joy in life. When we concentrate our soul efforts, we can merge with love and use that lens.

> *Will we still see some darkness and debris when we use that lens?*

Yes, because we are part of the collective consciousness, and we are responsible. Right now we have arrived at the time of consequences for humanity upon this earth. We have to face the consequences of our greed and grasping. We have reached a critical point which we could call crisis. But all over the world there are many who are working to stabilize, to remember, and to balance those forces of karma that we are all experiencing together. We have the choice to join these light workers and bring light and stability to this dimension. In this way, we are not overwhelmed by the darkness we see.

> *That which I am searching for is me.*
> *That which acts as an enemy is me, and that which is*
>   *attempting to get rid of the self-destructive me is also me.*
> *I am the obstruction and I am the way.*
> *That which obstructs is my own creation in unconsciousness.*

The 'I' that is the light of consciousness that removes the darkness of unconsciousness and ignorance is hiding behind unconsciousness.

That which I am searching for is hidden behind all the false images I hold of myself.

That which remains and cannot be removed after getting rid of all that I have acquired, is the real me (Yogi Amrit Desai).

All that we are is perfect.
All that we need has already been given.
Every moment is a time to observe from the
beautiful vantage point of consciousness - the
place where we merge in communion with the
resonance of God - the pure witness within.
Every moment is a time to let go, let go, let go
and realize the gift has already been given and
the blessing has already been bestowed.

5

THE PIVOTAL PRACTICE OF
WITNESS CONSCIOUSNESS

Our Connection to the Divine

Witness consciousness is available to you at all times. It is neutral and observes everything. Witness consciousness observes how you feel physically, it observes the quality of your emotions, and it observes the activity of your mind. We access witness consciousness through meditation.

> *Begin by closing your eyes and breathing deeply and slowly. As you breathe in and out consciously, the body and the mind begin to relax and to slow down.*
>
> *As you continue breathing for a few minutes, allow yourself to focus on the sound of your breath and any sensations that you may feel. Be neutral. Do not judge any sensation or thought or feeling that is coming in. Let your awareness rise to the third eye. The third eye is above the eyebrows in the middle of the forehead. Your eyes are closed, and you bring your attention to this space and place within you. Continue to breathe, becoming more relaxed and more peaceful.*

Once again, just observe everything from the place of the neutral observer. Allow and notice anything that arises in your feelings or your thoughts without making any adjustment or judgment, thereby allowing these energies to be neither expressed nor suppressed. They are simply allowed in the neutral space of witness consciousness.

The witness consciousness is your consciousness merging with the universal consciousness of God. When you succeed in quieting yourself with the breath, in focusing on the sound and sensation of the breath, and in feeling your energy ascend to your crown, you are merged with the consciousness of God. This pivotal practice creates peace and beauty within. Without merging with this resonance, stillness, and neutral love, you are resonating in your own personality.

The pivotal practice of witness consciousness allows us to ascend and to become neutral and peaceful, and yet it still allows everything around us to be as it is. Nothing is suppressed. From the witness consciousness, you feel everything you are feeling. Your thoughts are coming in and going out naturally. Witness consciousness is an inner practice, and if you do it, you are revealing yourself to your Self.

Witness consciousness brings you into God's vibration. In the midst of all the chaos of this dimension - the constant pulling back and forth - you find the neutral balancing point of the witness. Merging with this harmony stabilizes you. When you stabilize yourself through the practice of the breath, meditation, and witness consciousness, it positively affects everything in an unseen, powerful way.

Strive to mature and expand your consciousness so you can resonate with the resonance of God and realize beauty and peace. For this to happen, the seed willingness to control yourself and mature your emotional body must be nurtured and grown. Everyone unconsciously wants to engage in justification, questioning, judging, anger, frustration, and constant conversation. If you see that you are getting reactive about something, it is your responsibility to step back and ground that energy through the breath, and through witness consciousness. Witness consciousness can help you see, neutrally. When you cannot become neutral, then you are in one pole or another: *I am right, they are wrong, they are good, they are bad, I am not good enough, they are better than me, I agree, I disagree,* and so on. Veering from pole to pole can never change until you can sustain neutrality within. In the neutral consciousness of God, there is perfect equality of everyone and everything.

Let the seed willingness inside of you bring you to the witness within, over and over again. If you are a mature spiritual practitioner, you will not judge yourself for what you see because that judgment destroys your practice. If you observe yourself and you say, "Wow, I said something really unkind to that person" or "I am feeling so greedy about this," you cannot know peace and beauty. Peace and beauty are void of judgment. Do not use your observation against yourself; it is to be used in neutral, unconditional love so you can merge with the Holy Resonance.

Do you want to realize peace and beauty? If you do, it is there. *Thou art that.* It is within you. It always has been and always will be.

> *So when I observe that I'm having an unkind thought,*
> *or that I'm angry, or whatever, what do I do?*

Witness it first, and then breathe into it. Witnessing it first and consciously breathing into it with long, deep breaths, stabilizes the neutral witness. You notice it, you observe it, and you are neutral. *It arises, it is, it dissolves:* This is the practice of the witness. You are upset, and you are feeling it, but you notice it and you breathe into it. You are neutral; there is no judgment.

The energy of your thoughts and emotions can release like a wave; the wave comes in and then the wave goes out. It is not a complex head process. The breath *is* the fire. The breath is doing all the work, and you are sitting in the fire. Sit there, and breathe, breathe, breathe, and be in witness consciousness. This is *not* an intellectual process of figuring things out.

> *What if it's a karmic pattern that keeps coming back,*
> *one that I don't seem to be able to neutralize? Do I stay*
> *with it?*

Yes, over and over again, whenever the pattern comes up. That is the practice of engaging the witness consciousness in meditation. A good analogy is how we might practice an exercise to stay in shape physically. A repeated action eventually results in toned muscles and greater strength. In spiritual practice, when you return and return again and become neutral, you are maturing your emotional and mental bodies. As this maturation takes place, distressing emotions and thoughts naturally start to dissolve.

Is there a difference between meeting ourselves in meditation, as opposed to meeting ourselves out in the "real world"?

No, it is all the same. It is like yoga. There is on the mat, and there is off the mat. We go on the mat to learn how to do postures and to breathe consciously into what is tight and rigid in our bodies; we strive to soften and open. The purpose of yoga is to translate what we have learned *on* the mat into when we are *off* the mat. Yoga is about our internal consciousness everywhere, at all times.

Likewise, if you are sitting in meditation and a fear arises, or if you are driving down the road and a fear arises, what you do about it is the same. You breathe and open.

However, the witness consciousness is not the same as a pose in yoga. Witness consciousness *is* the consciousness of God. It is the part of us that is connected to the divine. That is beyond words.

Return to Beauty

That which I am searching for is me.
That which acts as an enemy is me, and that which is
attempting to get rid of the self-destructive me is also me.
I am the obstruction and I am the way.
That which obstructs is my own creation in unconsciousness.
The 'I' that is the light of consciousness that removes the
darkness of unconsciousness and ignorance is hiding
behind unconsciousness.

That which I am searching for is hidden behind all the
false images I hold of myself.
That which remains and cannot be removed after getting
rid of all that I have acquired, is the real me (Yogi
Amrit Desai).

We have been talking about how to ascend into the neutral and loving witness consciousness. Witness consciousness brings you into *tapas*, the transformation of what is heavy or agitated, into lightness of being. The way to do this is to keep returning to the witness. Whatever you see, let go. If you see it is hard to let go, accept yourself and do not go into self-rejection. Avoid blaming someone or something outside of yourself for the blockages you discover. Go through the whole process of allowing whatever it is that you have to let go of, to burn through; this is the surrender of *tapas*.

Appreciate whatever small steps you are able to take, moment by moment. Be grateful for a mini-victory. Let go of an unrealistic desire for completion and be patient with the process. Every time you become impatient or frustrated, return your attention and commitment to the witness consciousness. Return again and again to the power of the breath. Whatever you witness is about *you*; it is not about anyone or anything else. This understanding is the doorway to peace and self-realization.

Purification

It is difficult not to be affected by the times we are living in. These times are so challenging and burdensome, and change is happening so rapidly, that we cannot process it all. On top of all that, there is the microcosm of your life. You get up in the morning and go through your day. What do you do about all the things that continually arise during the day? The spiritual warrior must abide in the consciousness of purification. This is not purification in the sense of, "Something inside of me is bad," but this is purification in the positive sense of allowing yourself to let go of the debris and dusting yourself off from your perception of external insults that you suffer daily in this world.

How do you shed the debris daily so you are purifying and able to let go into *tapas*? *Tapas* is purification; it is the constant return to the witness to allow yourself to purify so you can find lightness of being, turn the lead into gold, and walk in beauty and peace. The purification process is constant, it is relentless. If you are not in the perpetual consciousness of love, it is easy to get backed up very, very quickly and get infected with what is not of God. It is easy to forget when you are upset, that your reaction is about you and you are the only one who has the power to return to the breath, to return to the witness, to release all judgment, and to burn your reaction in the fire of love.

We are living in times of change and consequence. The changes are happening relentlessly. It is easy to feel overwhelmed by it all. But you do not have to be concerned with processing it, or trying to make sense of it. All you need to be concerned with is your inner spiritual process and your relationship with God. All you need to do is abide there so that you are stable, beautiful, and fully alive.

The Quest: There is No Place to Go, There is Nothing to Do….

Is the witness consciousness the same as the soul? What is it that's watching us?

That is the question. What is it that is watching us? That is something for you to really explore through your own experience. Going into witness consciousness is bringing your awareness to a new place. This place is neutral. It does not judge, evaluate, draw conclusions, or make projections; it simply observes.

What is it observing? It is observing what is. That is why I always say, *it arises, it is, it dissolves.* Everything we think is so real, is not real. *It arises, it is, it dissolves.* That is the wave of emotions and thoughts. If you can observe them neutrally, they *arise*, you observe them, and then, if you sit with them and observe them long enough, they will *dissolve*.

But who is observing? Sit in witness consciousness, and witness yourself witnessing; see what you see. It is a wonderful, lovingly detached place where, if you can really arrive there through sustained practice and purification, you will never take yourself so seriously again because everything is changing all the time. Not to take yourself seriously is another way of saying you will not be so self-absorbed, but you will be much more attuned to the flow of light and love. You will be carried on these currents which are peaceful even when there are difficulties and challenges; there is a peace and steadiness there, no matter what is going on around you.

So your question is one that every spiritual warrior, seeker, or soul should explore. If I wanted to answer from the head, I would say that the witness is the part of our consciousness that merges with God. But those are just words. It is better to watch what you are feeling and thinking when you are practicing the witness. It is better in that expanded state of consciousness to observe what that feels like, what the qualities of the witness are, and to learn how to be swift in going there.

> *Sometimes my reactions are so quick that only after the*
> *fact do I remember to witness them.*

That is you thinking your reaction actually means something so you can tell yourself, "Oh, I didn't catch that, I wasn't quick enough." Just as quickly as the reaction is there, you can feel it and know instantaneously that this is the work. When your practice is sustained, your reactions turn into responses. Let us say your husband says something to you and it presses a button. You know *instantly* that your button is pressed, and you know *instantly* that you have a choice: Are you going to raise your voice, get frustrated and mad, or are you going to control yourself and breathe and be in witness? Find the fire to be beautiful. Find the fire to forge your life in every moment. You do not know how many moments you have; every one is a jewel, every one is so precious.

Even with all of the current events and other issues in our world, it is always the same. It comes back to personal responsibility and finding within yourself, what keeps your heart open so you can continue to love, feel, and find your own points of balance. It always comes back to being responsible for your thoughts, words, and deeds. It all comes back to that place. Nothing else is within your means to change, but you can change yourself, and when you do, it affects the whole.

People join organizations, go on marches, and participate in protests in order to bring about change. Some of that may be good, but it is seldom very effective. Issues become polarized: This is good, and that is bad. Then there is a fight, and that is war.

There is no place to go, there is nothing to do, and it takes everything you've got. You are already here, you are it, *Thou art that.* There is no new technique, there is no new channeled information. All of that may be interesting, but none of it is going to make any difference except to take you off point. It will not do the work for you, but sitting everyday in meditation will, living life as a prayer will, and living life as a meditation will. Saying thank you and being grateful every day will. All the really simple things will sustain you. The beauty that is all around us is astounding and so very sustaining. The heat of the fire is sustaining, the thirst-quenching water is sustaining, the food is sustaining; there is so much that sustains us. We are so blessed, so blessed.

The Gift is Given

The Lord is my shepherd, I shall not want . . . .

I shall not want is the essence of the Twenty-third Psalm. During the day, observe how much you want things to be different. If you want things to be different, you are not receiving the gift. She offers us everything in every moment. Wanting is the lead of life, not the gold. By accepting everything, we turn the lead into gold.

Everyone has the same freedom and the same choice to bring light into the situation. No one is outside of this freedom; it is your choice. But we miss the gift; you have to give the gift to yourself. Fill yourself with silence. Of all the talking we do, very little of it matters.

If you do not want anything, you are clear to receive God's inspiration; you can receive it and be used. God is not hard to find; God is a resonance. You receive your heart's desire when you move with the energy. One day consciousness becomes so stable that you shine and are uplifted in every moment.

This is everybody's gift, but hardly anyone receives it; everyone wants to be in control. It is not difficult to receive guidance and direction if you are open to receive the gift. The gift has been bestowed; it is already with you.

Perseverance is the continued effort to do or to achieve something despite difficulties, failure, or opposition. It is the single most important virtue in self-realization.

The simple act of returning again and again to consciously breathe and enter into stillness, is the great sustainer. It is nourishment of the soul at the deepest level.

As we go deep in meditation, the energy begins to inwardly expand. As our consciousness is brought deeper within, we can feel and find and know what is within us. And if what is within us is allowed to come forth, it can save our lives. Going deeply within can feel challenging, but it is the best way for revealing to ourselves, our selves. It is the best way to feel and know our union and communion with the great mystery.

CHAPTER

6

ANCHORED, CENTERED EMPOWERMENT

Harnessing the Pure Energy of Consciousness

The purpose of being on a spiritual path is to be in conscious relationship with the soul and therefore, in union with the divine. In order for the union to take place successfully, one practices self-reflection and self-observation without judgment. This is witness consciousness.

The witness is the only place from which you can look at yourself and observe all that you are. From the witness, the full spectrum of all the poles you are expressing — comfortable/uncomfortable, angry/patient, positive/negative — can be observed without judging whether they are right or wrong, good or bad. Witness consciousness embodies the absolute.

As you practice witness consciousness within, you can then begin to practice as you look outside of yourself toward others. This is the basis for conscious relationship. You can either be a compassionate mirror for others, or you can receive a mirror for yourself. You can stay in a neutral, loving, and compassionate place as you give or receive.

Let us say a man is frustrated with his wife. He feels he responds to most of her needs and wants, and yet, she never acknowledges this or says thank you. In fact, not only does she not say thank you but she also complains to him about his inattentiveness. Over time his frustration has mounted and so he very often feels himself in emotional reaction.

It is at this juncture that the internal process has a chance to be transformed. The set up appears to him that *she* is the reason for his frustration. Her behavior is his justification to feel angry and frustrated. However, as he begins to self-reflect and realize that he cannot change her behavior, only his own, then the door of consciousness can open and inner transformation can begin to take place. In the moment of frustration he can accept the reaction he is feeling is his own. He can then go through the internal process of watching, through the witness, what is arising while bringing the breath to the forefront and simultaneously feeling all the sensations of frustration. ***It is. It arises. It dissolves.*** The breath begins to neutralize the reaction.

When you take the blame off of a person or situation outside of yourself and simply, without judgment, take responsibility for your feelings, a huge release of potential, projected energy happens. This potential energy is now available for creative purposes.

As you practice this internal discipline, transformation is taking place. When you observe, without judgment, what is limiting you, you can let it go. This transforms the limitations of the ego that prevent the evolution of the soul. If you enter into self judgments such as "I should know better by now," or "I'm not able to do that yet," you block the possibility of seeing how you are limiting yourself. But if you are in witness and you stay neutral, without judgment, you can see how you limit yourself. Over time, the limitations are revealed and dissolved.

The path of transformation is to tread one step at a time as you witness and release whatever keeps you from union with your own soul. First, practice within yourself and make progress by bringing the witness to all situations with all people. When a challenging situation occurs between you and someone else, it is a divine set-up, an opportunity orchestrated for the possibility of your spiritual transformation. These set-ups come when least expected, when you feel most vulnerable. Under these circumstances you are greatly tested. It is easy to let go when it feels like not much is at stake. It is much more difficult to let go when it feels like everything is at stake.

To see the set-up will establish an opening for transformation. Once the situation is recognized as a set-up, you will realize that it is not about a person or situation. That person or situation is playing a role for you, and those set-ups are designed to bring you exactly where you need to be so you can feel exactly what you need to feel and learn. It is not about the external situation or person you are relating to. It is internal. Understand that it is about you and your own soul.

The possibility for consciousness lies within that moment. That moment is your point of power. When someone plays a role for you, it stimulates the possibility for this transformation to occur. As your fear, insecurity, judgment or anger is revealed, it becomes possible in that moment to open to pure consciousness as you release the obstacle that keeps you from the light of God. In that moment, purification of fear, insecurity, judgment or anger is taking place.

A shift in consciousness happens when you choose empowerment, when you allow your insecurities to be purified. It may feel as if you are losing power because the ego does not feel gratified and strong. The ego feels defeated and weak, but in reality, your soul is gaining strength.

When you play with the power of anger, you feel as if you have control. The sheer force of anger easily manipulates people and situations. With anger comes the illusion of power and control, but anger will not give you the experience of anchored, centered empowerment. To find real empowerment, you must allow yourself to go to the opposite pole, which is being powerless, and allow spirit to be at the helm.

When you enter into the release and purification of anger, a creative, constructive energy begins to be realized. Anger is fueled by fear of the unknown, fear of loss of control, and fear of vulnerability. When these filters of fear are removed, the same potential for energy exists. When the power that fueled the anger is void of the negative distortion, it is now free to be experienced and expressed as a constructive, creative force that embodies healthy empowerment. Paradoxically, surrender, release of control, and acceptance pave the way for pure energy to be harnessed. Learning how to harness this energy engenders the creative process. The energy is always accessible and can even gain in momentum once the distorting filters are no longer blocking its path.

Energy is infinite. It is only experienced as limited when you try to control it or when you try to own it by holding onto it. Your energy body expands beyond your physical body; it is fueled by *prana,* the infinite, inexhaustible energy of the universe. It is the never-ending source of energy and empowerment that sustains us. By consciously allowing purification of the ego, and therefore development of your soul, you can tap into this source because there is nothing in you resisting it. When there is nothing in you that resists, the energy flows fully and effortlessly. Then you experience integration, empowerment, and union.

This spiritual practice - choosing empowerment through the witness, even in the most challenging of circumstances - is an ongoing practice. Through life's trials and tribulations, you are constantly given opportunities to choose consciousness. The opportunities never stop, but as you become more adept at the practice, the load lightens. If the purpose of being on a soul path is transformation, which is soul realization and union with the divine, then every step you take strengthens your spiritual muscles. When you become adept at meeting all that life brings to you without complaint and with gratitude, then you will realize this source has always been and always will be feeding your every move and your every breath. To say, "Thy will be done, not mine," brings empowerment.

Practices for a Good and Simple Life

In spiritual awakening there is a gradual unfolding of deeper and more subtle awareness. All of the impulses that come to you, come from spirit. There is not a thought that is your own. Spirit individuates through each one of us as we express ourselves.

Nothing outside of you is outside of spirit. In other words, everything that comes to you comes from spirit. With this realization, the need to control the situations in life, and the fear of not doing the right thing will begin to dissolve. As you build trust in spirit, serendipitous and synchronistic events happen more frequently. Being in the right place at the right time is the result of trusting this awareness. All of the infinite energy of the universe is now available to you. It is limitless and unbounded, and it is always there. By releasing the blocks and limitations of ego that keep you from the light of spirit, you accept the path of freedom.

These words sound good, but how do you remove these limitations and blocks? How do you ground these ideas into a practice that becomes the basis for a good and simple life? How do you surrender to spirit? First, hold the awareness that nothing is outside of spirit. When you feel a reaction to anyone or anything, know that your spiritual work is at hand. And then—

1. *Be in witness.* Allow yourself to see what arises. Neutrally observe, even if you are in pain or disharmony mentally, emotionally or physically. Relax your body. Let go. If you are reacting against something, you are out of center. As soon as your mind starts to argue or defend, return to the breath and relax. Return again and again to the neutral witness.

2. *Accept yourself when you see your weaknesses, and do not go into self-rejection.* Return to witness. So you get angry, so you are stubborn, and so you are self-righteous. You are not above or beyond these places; it is how you react to them that you must work with.

3. *Stop blaming someone or something outside of yourself.* Own what is yours. When you see those places, own your anger, projections, and stubbornness, and they will then become your points of power.

4. *Sit with those feelings and let them burn through completely; that is tapas.* You have now been able to go into witness, you have seen your reaction, and you are going to own it. You still feel threatened and angry, or whatever. The energy is still there, but you are responding to the energy differently than you did before. *Tapas* is purification; it is active and it burns. You may feel heat; you may feel your heart pounding, your blood pumping, and any number of things as the emotion runs through you.

As you sit with it, you may still want to enlighten him or to show her that your way is better, but you do not, because you own what is yours. This is *tapas*. You want the world to know that you are right, and you are sure that you are right, but no one is ever going to know or care because you are going to burn up that self-righteousness. This is *tapas*. You are never going to be recognized for what you think you should be recognized for. This is *tapas*. You are never going to be understood in the way you feel you should be understood. This is *tapas*. You are never going to get what you feel you really deserve. This is *tapas*. Be humble. You just did something really big, and no one said thank you. This is *tapas*.

Sometimes it takes more time to let those places burn through, but we do not care. We stay with the stimulation until such time as we can let it go. We process it until we can return to peace.

5. *Be grateful for a small victory.* Be in appreciation for whatever small gains you are able to realize. Be content to do this humble work in a small but powerful way, in increments, as spirit sees fit to bring it to you. This is humility. This is the practice.

6. *Be patient with the process and let go of an unrealistic desire for completion.* Persevere. You have to be able to be willing to be incomplete and to be okay with both your shortcomings and strengths. You are a work in progress and have everything you need. Accept how you are right now; take it or leave it. If you do not take it, then you are resisting it. If you resist it, then you are doing battle with your own soul again and it comes back on you. You will lose all your precious and vital energy in this fight. You will have a drain of energy, and you will not know why. Allow yourself to be in the process. How you are in the moment is what you bring to it. Stand up front with all of your imperfections, and go forth.

The Fuel for Awakening

My practice all seems to be about the same old stuff.

You are recognizing and seeing the potential for healing that keeps showing itself to you over and over again. But when you say it is the same old thing, you are putting it in a place where you can trivialize it or feel victimized and unhopeful about it. Instead, see it as the fuel to build your fire of the desire to be beautiful and peaceful.

Keep accepting it. It is not over until it is over, and it does not matter how long the sequences last in life. It does not matter, even if it is life long or all the next life long. All that matters is that you say, "I'm sticking with it; however long it takes me, I'm sticking with it."

We pray to go from unconsciousness to consciousness. That is why we do not berate ourselves or allow ourselves to become frustrated with our failures. Most of our actions every day are generated from unconscious patterns. As people on a soul path, we know this. So we are not surprised when we do something and we think, "Wow, that didn't serve me very well. There's that old pattern again, another round for me."

Our failures are the fuel for awakening. When we see ourselves fail and it does not feel good, we get to self-reflect and to see how we have served ourselves or others, or how we have *not* served ourselves or others. We get to see those places so we can give ourselves a chance to do better.

Be grateful for the epiphanies that come to you and for the consciousness that opens to you. Never berate yourself when you fail. Enlightenment is in the moment that you bring light to it.

There is nowhere to go.
There is nowhere to hide.
There is nothing to do.
Abide in the gift of the present moment. Within
the moment of now, all is as it should be. There
are no exceptions to this universal law. Letting
go, into the full acceptance of now, brings peace,
openness, and therefore, love, into our hearts.
May no one be the least little bit unhappy, ever.

7

IN THE FACE OF SUFFERING

The Places that are Void of Suffering

If you were asked to take a moment to observe your choices in life through witness consciousness, what would you find? Do you still, from time to time, use the places you know do not serve you? Do you find yourself looking outside for validation, seeking control over events, and needing to grab and hold? All of these repetitive behaviors and patterns cause pain and suffering. Yet, somewhere inside, you still believe these shadow places can get you what you want—some attention, some security, or perhaps some protection.

Once you see that these places and patterns will not get you what you want, then you can start to let them go. When you *really* see it, you will not want to waste one more drop of your precious love going down those drains because they lead to nothing but suffering. They do *not* bring more security, they do *not* bring more control, they do *not* get people to help you, and they do *not* bring about a better self-image.

When you see that, you can start to invest your heart and soul in the places that do get you what you want: the cessation of suffering and peace within. The spirits of love, peace, beauty, and the spirit of the Lord God and of the Holy Mother are void of suffering. Turn the shadow places around by shining your light on them and seeing clearly that they are never, ever going to get you what you want.

The desire for something outside of ourselves can be so strong; take that deep desire and turn it toward your transformation, love, and healing. Take all the energy of that desire and let it flourish, be nourished and grow. This is when healing and light get amplified; it feels wonderful, it feels beautiful, it feels whole. *I will lift up mine eyes unto the hills, from whence cometh my help. My help cometh from the Lord, which made heaven and earth.* Call for help; the help is within.

If you invest in the spiritual dimensions and you use the spiritual laws, your investment will come back to you tenfold. This is where all the magic happens. This is where all of the synchronicity and magic of life live. If you know this, and hang on to it, you will always give yourself what you *really* want by going within.

At a time when many have forgotten, it is so important that those of you who do remember, do everything in your power to feed the remembrance of what is loving, peaceful, and kind. Very simply return to yourself by closing your eyes, breathing consciously, and entering the resonance of the still point, for the qualities of love, peace and beauty dwell within you.

Perfect Clarity in the Face of Suffering

People who are experiencing challenges and trials may or may not deserve them. We should not judge them. On a human or moral level, they may well be innocent; sometimes very good people suffer and such suffering appears to be unjust. The soul, however, deserves to experience the episodes it chooses. A person may need to disassemble for reasons of the soul.

Perhaps a person is suffering for the actions of another life time. All of us, in our multiple lifetimes, have killed other people, have ourselves been killed, have suffered terrible disease, have known destitution, have perpetrated and been perpetrated upon. We work through these events in one lifetime or another.

Many people suffer the same or similar calamities. Some of them recover while others do not. Why is this so? When a soul has its reasons, its progress cannot be stopped. We might yearn deeply to stop the track of unhappiness and the terrible dissolution that our friends and relatives experience. This yearning of ours does not assist them. Another possibility is for us to respect the path of the soul.

The suffering a person experiences does not end with itself. Even if they suffer for a lifetime or choose to end their life because of the extremity of their suffering, they will begin to assemble again. No matter what the extent of their disintegration may be, they are held by universal law and the light of God. They are held by the light and love of the universe. When they recognize where they are, when they recognize the strength of spirit, they will turn. Disassembly cannot end with itself. Assembly always follows disassembly.

If you identify your own suffering in the suffering of others, you begin to believe in their suffering with them. Then you are supporting their suffering, and you assist it by confirming its power. Your own fear vibrates with it and makes it stronger. Their suffering stimulates your memory of suffering, and together you intensify one another's suffering. This is what pity is.

When you no longer see yourself in their pain, your identity is not confirmed by their unhappiness. Then you experience compassion, a benevolent kindness that is detached from your own experience of suffering. This compassion knows no yearning and no conflict. You become a healing presence that heals simply by the presence of its own light, without effort. You can see deeply into the heart of the suffering person because you are not bound by fear, sorrow, memory or dread within yourself. You achieve perfect clarity without judgment of yourself or others. The potential for this awareness exists, not in the mind, but in the heart. The perfect clarity you can achieve is not a matter of understanding but of love. Then you are healing by holding the light of the absolute, and you are centered in that light. You will not need to do anything because the light will do its work through you. Then you will heal simply as you are: self-existing, self-fulfilling, and self-sustaining.

Holding the Light

I have suffered greatly on behalf of my family and their suffering. If I can get to a place where I do not react, where I do not suffer with them, will their suffering also quiet down?

Their suffering may or may not quiet down. Most likely you will continue to witness the humanity of your loved ones—their failures, their successes, and the ways in which they choose suffering over peace. It is important, however, to not vibrate in the suffering. If you vibrate in the suffering, you will feed it. You will actually add to the energy of suffering and to the consciousness that believes it is real.

There is a beautiful way to be compassionately present without being karmically involved. Look at the lives of the saints and humanitarians. How did they do it? How did Mother Theresa, Mahatma Gandhi and Martin Luther King, Jr., do it? How did Mother Theresa succeed in being among the suffering, the dying and the poor—those who were most in need—and not go under? She did not vibrate or resonate with their suffering; she resonated with the light of Christ.

When you resonate with this light, you actually hold the light. You develop an inner constancy where peace and beauty abide. You stay there, and hold that place within yourself. This is not a matter of saying or doing the right thing. It is simply a state of being that aligns itself with the consciousness of God. This constant light will be realized by those around you as a peaceful and beautiful reassurance.

You do not have the power to release others from their suffering, but you do have the power to hold the light. If others should want this light, they have the free will to choose it for themselves. You have the power to be an anchor for this light.

Healing is a State of Mind and Heart

I've been thinking about Helen who's 97 years old. She just fell out of bed and broke her leg. She's in a lot of pain, and her family is not here. She must be having to find so much courage within herself because it's really just between her and God right now.

What is true of Helen at 97 in a nursing home, alone and without family, is true of you and everyone else. It is between you and God; it is between her and God. She is in the same place that we all are in. The Kingdom of Heaven is within us. This life is an inner journey. We have the chance to learn how to connect to the divine. Each of those trials, tribulations, and challenges, gives us an opportunity to journey deeply within. The divine door is within, and it is always available for us to open. You can open it once in a while, or you can keep it open all the time.

We have the gift of practice and prayer until we take our last breath; it is a gift of remembrance, and we are given many, many opportunities to remember all our lives long. If you bring the consciousness of forgiveness, love, and hope into all things, absolutely at all times and under all circumstances, you will realize healing, *no matter what.* You cannot avoid the circumstances of life; you cannot avoid the challenges that come to you personally. Healing does not mean you do not break your leg. Healing does not mean that you do not die or get old. Healing is a state of mind and heart. That state of consciousness has nothing to do with the burdens of the flesh. Higher consciousness can be held in the most incredible circumstances and predicaments.

We remember God by becoming the lover, the giver, the one who understands, and the one who holds the light and gives it freely. This is a key, a beautiful, golden key that creates the cycle of grace. It brings back to you tenfold what it is that you impart to the world.

Human behavior is mostly habitual, repetitive, and unconscious. Bringing awareness to our thoughts, words, and deeds helps us to dissolve the repetitions and habits. As we let go of the old, we open to a new awareness. Each time, a brand new beginning is revealed.

CHAPTER

8

KARMIC PATTERNS IN RELATIONSHIPS

Healing and Transforming Relationships

The relationships you have and the reactions you have to your relationships are generated within. How you react or respond to the stimulus that is provided by those relationships has everything to do with your inner level of consciousness. When a disagreement arises, the first thing the ego wants to do, is to blame the other person's attitude, impatience, or lack of understanding. The truth is, whatever is stimulated in you by those various scenarios, is your own karmic pattern. It is yours. It is very challenging in the midst of a frustrating or difficult situation to stop and quickly go within and not repeat the pattern that you always repeat.

We do not have any control over other people, but how we respond to the stimulus from someone else has a great impact on our relationship. When I was a young woman, I habitually responded to my mother with impatience, defensiveness, and frustration. I did not want to hear anything she had to say, and I did not agree with anything she said. From my perspective, she was relentlessly mean. There came a time when I no longer wished to live with the feelings that brought me such unhappiness with every conversation and every interaction.

What happens when we arrive at this point? Some people will just get out of the relationship. They will cut the family off, get a divorce, or just withdraw and shut everything down. When I saw how habitually unhappy my anger and resentment were making me, I felt compelled to find a way to become more peaceful. I entered into a healing process that empowered me and allowed me to bring forth the consciousness that I wanted to embody.

Because the stimulus coming to me from my mother was always the same, I had to learn how *not* to respond in my same way. This is not easy because the karmic pattern resides in the emotional body, and your emotional body is strongly responsive to the stimulus from another. You have to mature your emotional body by allowing yourself to be guided by your soul. Your soul will tell you, "This is you again, doing the same thing over and over again." You will swear that the other person is the cause of your frustration, but no, it is you. Wherever you go, there you are. You cannot get away from yourself. You can change relationships, you can marry different people, you can take new jobs, but if you sit in one place long enough, your pattern will come right back at you, over and over. It is relentless.

We must identify our perpetual karmic reactions and be grateful for the places that challenge us the most, because these places are teaching us. This stimulus helps us to bring light to what we do all the time. It is at this time, when it is the hardest, that we have the greatest potential to change.

Whenever I called my mother, the first thing she would say was, "What do you want? Why don't you come and see me? You're calling me, so you must want something." And off we would go into a fight. I would become angry and defend myself.

When I learned to say, instead, "So, you want to see me, Mom?" I would feel the softness, instantly.

"Well, yes, that would be nice."

"I know, I haven't seen you lately and haven't been able to come down much." She became softer. As long as I did not try to hold my position and defend myself, and as long as I mirrored her and what she was saying to me, I did not really have to do anything. There was nothing to do except release my position and ego, and thereby stop the fight. From that point on, our relationship became better and better until it transformed into the blessing of my life.

Not all of your karmic interactions are going to transform into the blessing of your life, but they are blessings, and they are privileges. We human beings do things backwards. We have to understand that we have to flip the situation over. If you think there is a problem out there, there is a problem in here. On the path of love, this is *Consciousness 101*.

The Commitment to Unhappiness

Places in you are deeply committed to crisis, sadness, and frustration—deeply committed! Your emotional body is so committed to feelings of misery that it will do almost anything to feel this way. It wants to prove to itself that there is a reason to be sad, a reason to be mad, a reason to be hurt, and a reason to retreat. The ego feels that way. Your soul, however, knows it is not true. The soul has no position. It accepts everything and unifies everything, even discord. As long as your soul is driving your vehicle, you will be reminded, whenever you feel justified in those feelings, that this is the work. This is the red flag saying, "This is it, this is where I work, this is what I do, this is it, now."

No matter how much work you have done and or how strong you feel in your spiritual self, there are places in your emotional body that are deeply committed to sadness, frustration, and anger. You only feel right when those places are present. This feels natural, and so it unconsciously likes to perpetuate indulging in those emotions. You are so committed to its naturalness as part of your identity, that you are willing to say, "Well, this is who I am, this is my nature." The soul wants you to be living in your true nature, but the ego will actually use your spiritual insights to defend its position, so you have to be very careful. If you are not honest and truthful with yourself, you will lie to yourself, and you will accept that lie.

*Yesterday I said something that was part of my pattern
of criticism. When my partner reacted, I said, "Well, get
used to it, I am who I am." I observed myself justifying it,
but I couldn't let it go; I was completely committed to it.*

This is a good example of how we use a spiritual argument to defend ourselves. It is good for us to know our true nature as a human being, but not to use it as a spiritual defense mechanism; that really destroys our path and our practice. When a spiritual principle is used in defensiveness, it is just another ego reaction.

If we could really digest how committed we are to perpetuating our unhappiness, we could begin to see it better and neutralize it more quickly and waste less precious time holding it in place.

Do not think you can free yourself from your karmic patterns by continually switching teachers and teachings. "I'll do this class, this meditation, and then I'll go over here and I'll get certified in such and such, and then I'll read this book and go into that training." None of that will work. The new territory may relieve the pressure initially because you may feel there is some new understanding. That feels good for a little while, but eventually even that gets peeled away, and there you are again.

Be honest with yourself, and admit when you are fully in your pattern and committed to your position and unhappiness. The single most effective thing at those times is the breath. Just breathe to give yourself thirty seconds, sixty seconds, or two minutes to *not* respond in the perpetual way. Right then, at that moment, breathe. Right then, say "This is it. This is about me."

As I became less defensive with my mother, there was less to defend when my pattern was activated with her. I began to feel more balance and more harmony inside myself.

No one can take anything away from you. No one can take away your happiness. Nobody can do it. Nobody can take away your inner harmony unless you stay deeply committed to your own unhappiness and you give it away. Then you either blame the person out there, or you blame the person in here. Either way, both of these positions will make you unhappy.

What really brings happiness is the inner peace and harmony that comes about when we are not feeding negative patterns and are staying neutral in witness consciousness and practicing the breath. As we come to see our shortcomings and understand that we have karmic patterns that feed the ego, we can begin to stop feeding those patterns. Do not feed them.

Bapuji said, *May no one be the least little bit unhappy, ever.* When you are committed to unhappiness and are suffering, understand you can quickly bring in light and lift yourself. Only **you** can lift yourself. Then it does not matter what you are doing; it does not matter if you are scrubbing the toilet bowl or if you are taking a beautiful hike, if you are cooking or if you are at work. None of it matters; it is all the same then. Every task is equal; one is not harder than the other. It is all the same because there is no resistance. Your level of unhappiness is equal to your level of resistance. What you resist, persists. When you are resisting someone or something, you are absolutely experiencing a level of pain.

There are times in life when the pure action is to move forward in a different way, but that is not done out of reaction. It is done out of a simple, clear choice that it is time to move. Maybe it is time to get a new job because you need more stimulation, or maybe you feel that you have completed a project or a goal. That is not done in reaction; that is done in growth. And, people do reach the end of their contracts in relationship; they have fulfilled them and it is time to move on. But being able to acknowledge it consciously and complete it peacefully is very different from doing it out of ego defensiveness. One is done in harmlessness, and the other is done in unhappiness.

It will be Revealed

My former husband would take me back in a heartbeat.
Am I supposed to go back and make it right?

Not necessarily. Whenever we have a new awareness, it is good to let that awareness just seep into us and not react right away. It is much too quick to say, "Oh well, if it is all me and I can change myself, then I can go back." Instead, be with the new awareness that is coming in about who you are and understand that you have this power to always be in transformation, and then you will see what happens naturally. You can begin to see the relationship naturally change, positioned exactly as you are, in the moment.

Stay with yourself in the process, and then whatever is to be, will be revealed without your making reactionary decisions that perpetuate your unhappiness. *There's no place to go, there's nothing to do, and it takes everything you've got.* Sustain yourself with your soul while these new insights and epiphanies are coming in.

When you are on the path and start to see how you create unhappiness, you are very close to never being "the least little bit unhappy, ever." You are very close to being able to turn around the unhappiness inside and begin to feel your sacredness. You see, the sacredness of everything is the happiness. It is the sacredness of our own self, your inner temple of light, that you carry within. Then share that light and happiness in all of your interactions and with every step you take. Beauty is all around you, all about you, and within you, all the time.

Choose Love

At various times you have talked about surrendering positions, opinions and even preferences. I'm finding that preferences are not so lightweight. You recently gave the example of one person wanting to go the mountains, and one wanting to go to the ocean. My husband likes to keep the shades drawn; I like to keep them raised. For years we have argued about that.

Then you must create a sanctuary in your home where, when you go into that room, the lights are bright, the shades are up, and it has all the energy you want and need. Perhaps you have a conversation where you agree that one area can be more shaded, and then another area that is a common area, has to have more light. You compromise and then you create the sanctuary you need. It does not have to be a big debate because when you start to debate, you start going back and forth and it turns into a fight.

Could you be happy having a room that is filled with light, could you be happy having a shared space in the communal living area that has some light coming in and another part that doesn't?

Well, yes; I can agree to that, but it is not what I want.

It is not about what you want. When my mother Mary was here, I did not want to listen to the TV all the time. But what was more fulfilling for me was that she was happy. Sometimes I would lose my patience, and I must have called out, "Mute!" a million times when the commercials came on. But the most important thing was for us to be together and for her to be in a secure and supportive place during her time of transition. You have to remember the larger purpose of what you are doing.

I am not saying that there might not be times when we must do what we feel deeply we need to do. In times of crisis, for example, we might be guided to take a certain step. At those times we act out of clear light, and not out of defensiveness. But most of the time, the things that we are fighting about have no significance; it is just about our internal ego struggle.

We get so wrapped up in our fears and our unhappiness. These patterns are rigid. They are hard, crusty, and deeply grooved. Your disagreement about the shades is more about your reaction than anything else. It is all internal. The external things are the stimulus for the soul to do its work. All the circumstances are just that—an opportunity to choose love. What is the loving place? What brings in love?

There is a way for you to do that. There is a way to bring in the energy you need, and also be accepting of the other, simultaneously. We are not always in agreement with one another in our relationships. That is okay. I am not saying, "When we agree, then we'll be happy."

When we are in a loving place, we may not be in agreement, but we are free within ourselves and we are not trying to direct someone else to be another way other than the way they are. That will never happen. But as long as you think somebody else can keep happiness from you, then you have given them the power to do so, and so they can. It is not because they really wanted to do it; it was because you agreed to it.

May no one be the least little bit unhappy, ever, applies precisely to the example of the mountains or the ocean. The relationship is really about having a shared experience, and surely you can open your heart to that. And look at the odds—the mountains or the ocean? What is there to be unhappy about?

The divine flow is waiting for you to merge with its essence. The divine flow is waiting for you to discover yourself as soul. As you discover yourself as soul, you realize **you** *are the divine flow.*

This is a great mystery that reveals the amazing desire of the soul, which longs to give freely because its natural state of consciousness is to give. As you merge with the divine essence and begin to give and love, you unlock the door to the cycle of grace. All is received and all is given in an endless circle of blessing.

CHAPTER
9
THE CONSCIOUS SELF IS THE WAY

The Divine Door

Thou art that. Your essence is divine. The path of love is not exclusive; it is for everyone. We all have the same, amazing circuitry which allows us to navigate in the realms of the Holy Spirit. The heart is the doorway to the divine. The heart is the doorway to the feeling center. The feeling center is directly connected to divine impulse or guidance. Every moment is brand new. Every moment is an opportunity to have your heart's desire revealed to you.

Huge currents of life wash upon you in many ways. They frequently test and challenge you. When these waves come, *be still*. Just take a moment to become still and go within. In this stillness, your light body can register the impulses, and you can then intuit how these impulses are guiding you. Your intuition allows you to receive inspiration, ideas and insights as well as impulses that arrive as blockages or dead ends. The inspirations are green lights that say *yes*, and the blockages are red lights that say *no*. As you receive this information, you come into direct relationship with personal guidance. This is your empowerment, and you can return to this center over and over, moment by moment, to be guided in trust and love to your heart's desire. *Spirit wants for you what you want for yourself.*

Everything depends on the light. Your physical body is energized by your light body. Go within, be still, breathe deeply, and you will activate the light body, which in turn, nourishes the physical body. The light creates vitality and health.

The light will strengthen your aura, sealing off the holes of anger, greed, jealousy, and fear. As these holes are sealed and you become whole, you gain and sustain the strength to withstand the inevitable waves of life. This strength has its roots in your own divinity. *Thou art that.* You are already that which you are seeking. You already have everything you need. You just need to return, and return again, to the door of your own heart.

Whatever burden you are carrying, put it down. You do not have to carry it. Give it to the Mother. Return and return again to that which you already are. She has you. Find this resonance and let it open your heart to peace and love. It is the essence of the beauty of the rose. The perfection of color, configuration, and intoxicating scent is what you are. Place a rose on your altar, and during meditation and prayer time, take time to drink in its beauty.

You are trusting love when you hold this center. Anything around you can disassemble and reassemble. Everything changes. The one constant is the ever present golden center of the rose within your own heart. You are divine. See with divine eyes. Speak with divine words. Hear with divine ears. Work with divine hands and feel with your divine heart. The divine door is within you.

Lead Us from Darkness to Light

Asatoma sad gamaya,
Tamasoma jyotir gamaya,
Mrityorma amritam gamaya.

In the *Asatoma* prayer, we pray to be led from darkness to light, from untruth to truth, and from mortality to immortality. The prayer is six thousand years old, and all the masters of the East have used that prayer to help themselves open the door to the heart. The heart is connected to that from which we came, which is love, which is God, which is the frequency of the One.

On a really simple level, we can go through life in one of two ways, consciously or unconsciously. Which way is easier? It is easier, much easier, to be unconscious! In unconsciousness we do not have to sort out self and other. When we are unconscious, we perceive reality as our small selves, and everything else is outside of ourselves. That is how we see it with our two eyes. We can only perceive oneness when we close our two eyes and ignite the singular, third eye and go within; then we start to realize oneness from within.

What is the trigger that helps you to go from unconsciousness to consciousness? Quite simply, you do not feel good; you are suffering somehow. Something inside is stimulating you to find a way to do something differently from the way you have been doing it. Sometimes it is physical. "I feel sluggish, so I'm going to start exercising." Or "I've been eating junk and I haven't been feeling good, so I'm going to start eating a healthy diet." All of that is part of going from unconsciousness to consciousness. You notice something about yourself that you need to do differently, so you start to exercise or change your diet. On yet another level, you might have to face up to the fact that you are an alcoholic and go to AA for the first time. Or, you may feel desperate because something in your life is not working and has to change, so you make an appointment to see a therapist.

In time, after all the programs and self-help, you find that something is still missing. You are still suffering on some level. Something within you longs for that from which it came. It is like trying to fill an endless hole. We try to fill the hole with anything we can think of. We try this, and then we try that, over and over again. We try to fill the hole so we can find the satisfaction or contentment we long for. Even when we have all the external things that should be making us happy, we cannot fill the endless hole from outside of us.

In essence, that which we are, is calling us home. It will not let us go until we return within again and again in a deep, meaningful way that sustains our hearts and souls. Then we can find the flow, which is love, and live in the flow and be guided.

The desire to merge with that from which we came eventually leads us to spiritual awareness and we begin our search for God. God takes many shapes and many forms. Because we humans have a desire to crystallize, compartmentalize, and draw boundaries within which we can live and feel comfortable, we create religions and all of their various expressions. God can be Jesus Christ, God can be Buddha, God can be the Divine Mother, God can be Krishna, and so on. But it is all one.

When I talk about God, I am talking about a resonance. I am talking about a frequency of vibration that is unified as one. It is oneness. I often say God or Goddess because most people can relate to those somehow.

After you have been on a spiritual path for a while, you begin to find there are steps and stages on the path just as there are steps and stages in exercise and diet. After a few weeks or months, or even a few years on a healthy diet, you might decide to change your diet to a new one you think is even healthier than the first one you chose.

Your spiritual path is no different. "I've been meditating, doing yoga, doing this and that, and I'm stuck. After all I've done, is this all there is?" Who has not felt that? After all those years of eating well, staying physically fit, doing the inner work, and living in a good way, why do you come back around to, "Is this all there is?"

> *Because whatever we're doing is limited. I mean, it is not God. There has to be some additional opening somewhere.*

Yes, there has to be some additional opening somewhere. Somehow, you have fallen into the groove again. It is called karma.

> *Or ego?*

Ego and karma could be synonymous. As long as you think *you* are in charge and as long as *you* are driving the car, you are going to get stuck again in the karmic groove. You progress on the spiritual path; you meditate, pray, and go on retreats to deepen your practice. You do all that, but when push comes to shove, you do not surrender to God because you know best how things should be in your life, and you end up back in the same place.

> *But sometimes you don't even see that you're doing that.*

You do if you are really watching, but when guidance comes around, you often do not want to hear it. Why? Because you want things to be the way *you* want them to be. That desire will always be there, just like the thoughts in your head when you are meditating. Thoughts are always going to arise and drift through your awareness. Even when you are willing to practice surrendering and listening to guidance, you will still feel resistance. It is natural; it is a part of our humanness. That resistance keeps you in the karmic loop and does not want to let you go.

Your level of pain is equal to your level of resistance. The degree to which you can release resistance is the degree to which you can realize a simple, beautiful flow.

Look for the signs. There are always signs, signals and stepping stones in front of you. They show you where the next step is. You do not have to know the big picture. We never know that anyway. All you have to do is take the next small step.

Your fear creates the feeling of being overwhelmed because you think you are alone, without any help or support. You think you generate all the pieces and parts that are needed to make a change or do something in a new way. You feel this way until you find the flow, and then realize, "Oh, it's all happening already!"

The resonance will guide you, and the resonance is simple. Knowing God is not necessarily about having a vision of God while meditating in a cave somewhere. Knowing God is recognizing what feels open. Does this feel open? There is God. Does this feel closed? God is not there. If it is clear and feels open and light, it is a YES. If it is not all yes, and there is some contraction, it is a yellow or red light. Do not proceed. If it is a green light, take the step to the next stepping stone.

What is a conscious life? What does it mean to live consciously? In a conscious life, you open the door of your heart to the energy, resonance, and light from which it came. You are guided and loved in a way far beyond your wildest dreams, beyond what you could ever imagine, manipulate, or make up for yourself. Magic happens because it is not you, in your small self, trying to make it all happen. It is you merging with the God self from which you came, and allowing yourself to be guided into that flow.

The Conscious Self Surrenders Everything

In rare moments, you drop your wants, needs and fears. Pettiness and the insistence on having things your own way dissolves. In the empty space of the dissolution, room is made for the true nature of love to fill you. You need nothing. You are relaxed and your self-consciousness disappears. You are in the divine current. It feels as natural as breathing in and out. You are open.

Bu what happens? The wall of the self returns. Your agenda, which is a pre-determined, automatic response to how you meet life, rears its ugly head and demands you to **not** open, and **not** change. You close down and shut the door.

You set up roadblocks to the flow of life by pushing, pulling, manipulating and being attached to outcomes. The moment you attempt to make something happen the way you want it to, you get in the way and the current is lost. The moment you act on your own behalf, you distance yourself from love. Any attempt that is made to manipulate, alter, force, reject or attain anything, splits the energy and separates you from union with divine love.

Separation impacts every level of your being: physical, emotional, mental and spiritual. In a state of separation, the body is constantly unwell. We feel physically limited and imposed upon by the body. We have no vitality, no energy. Even if we are well, we do not feel well if consciousness is blocked. Emotionally, we are in a state of reaction against our experience: "Yes, I like it," or "No, I don't like it." We position ourselves as to what we like and want or do not like and want. We resist what is. On the mental level, we question, doubt, and analyze. We are terrorized by a restless mind that is never satisfied. Spiritually, we feel separated, isolated, cut off, and empty.

In a state of union, on the other hand, the body is harmonious, filled with vitality and energy. Even if physical disease is present, a sustaining level of acceptance and flow exists if consciousness is *not* blocked. Emotionally, we accept what is given to us in life, and we feel grateful. We divest ourselves of preferences and become open and responsive to what is. On the mental level, the questioning stops. The mind is open to possibility, and we wait on the will of heaven. On the spiritual level, we feel connected, unified, and complete.

With these checkpoints, it is easy to see whether you are open or closed. With the spiritual practice of self-reflection, you can learn to see the differences quickly and grasp what triggers consciousness or unconsciousness. Meditation and conscious breathing dissolve the individual self that is dissatisfied and full of cravings. The unconscious self is an obstacle. The conscious Self is the way. If you choose fear and doubt, they are yours. If you choose simplicity and liberation, they are yours. The unconscious self has agendas, preferences, obsessions, and opinions. The result is frustration and unfulfilled outcomes. The conscious Self surrenders everything and attempts nothing. The result is simplicity and a life of realized blessings and unexpected joys.

Succeeding in Practice

> *I don't feel the enthusiasm that I should for practice and meditation. I do it, but usually I have to make myself sit down and do it. My practice seems to go deeper and become more meaningful when there is a crisis at hand.*

What you are saying is, "My practice is a 'should' right now, but something is pressing upon me to change it." Spiritual practice does not need to be more than a sense of knowing it is good for you. It is a discipline. If you understand it as a discipline, it can be a simple, peaceful experience. It is not necessarily ecstatic in the beginning, or even much later after years of practice. Ecstasy is a promise for hanging out in peaceful places. If you do it enough, you are bound to realize more ecstatic frequencies and places.

It is a misconception that we need a crisis. It is best to sustain practice when all is well. Then, when the crisis comes, we are much more prepared. Until you break through the wall of your self, your simple, peaceful practice will continue as it is. But it could become an empty ritual, which is what often happens in religious practice. What do you bring to the container of your practice? When one wants to succeed, one can.

Fanning the Flame of Your Desire

If you desire to know God, and that desire is pure, you must find a way to fan that flame. When you do, your heart creates the connection that is always there and waiting. It is always there. You do not have to wait to see if it is going to happen. It is happening in every moment; it is *happening* as we speak.

You are waiting to see how much this connection means to you. How much do you want it? Is this your heart's desire? Your desire has to be aligned with a passionate intention that is part of your own soul. The soulful self knows the bliss, lives in the bliss, and is the bliss.

You can meditate and do all the spiritual practices and never change a thing. You have to *bring* something to meditation and spiritual practice. That something is your heart and soul. What you bring into it at the beginning is what you will take away at the end.

When I was a novice, I was attending *satsang* at Kripalu. There were 400 people in the temple with Gurudev on the harmonium and others playing instruments. People would be going crazy, dancing and chanting! I would be thinking, *I don't get it.* Then one day Gurudev said, *If you hold back, you will have a held-back experience.* Then I got it. I was going in and holding back. When I went in again, I closed my eyes and let the energy take me into the chant and dance.

Do the same thing with your practices. Go within and surrender to the energy. Do not analyze it: "Do I feel OK? Do I feel anything at all? What is the person next to me feeling?" None of that matters. Go within.

There are many practices that help us to develop our inner channel of light. We are so crusty and hard. Sometimes it is difficult to feel we can ever get over ourselves. But we can, we really can. *Tapas* ignites the yogic fire, which is the light of God, and brings it through our practice so the fire burns up all resistance. The light knows what the light is doing. All you have to do is let the light in.

As you move and breathe through each day, cultivate the willingness to be kind to yourself. Self-reflection is a powerful tool. It reveals all aspects of the self and the Self. When a flaw is unveiled, make no judgment. Do not slip down into shame. Be willing to meet your shortcomings in the spirit of fearlessness and remember that this willingness to transform comes from a place of goodness within you. When a flaw is unveiled in another, make no judgment. Do not slip down into blame. In the same spirit of fearlessness, be compassionate. We all have shortcomings, and we are all good.

CHAPTER

10

COMMITTING TO
SPIRITUAL GROWTH

Lessons in Earth School

It was the first day of school, and I was only five years old. I did not
know the teacher or any of the other children. Mrs. Stinson asked
each one of us to say our names and to say what our fathers did for
work. I listened carefully. It did not take me long to realize that I did
not know what my father did, but I knew enough to make something
up that sounded like all the other fathers' professions. So I said my name
and then, "my father works in a store." Mrs. Stinson looked down at
me with disdain. "He does no such thing, young lady. It says here that
he is a machinist!"

I distinctly remember the feeling of heat rising up through my chest
and into my face. The closest place I could find to hide was in the small
desk in front of me. I bent over and pushed my face into the opening as
far as I could. I had been embarrassed and humiliated in the very first
hour of my very first day of school.

On that day I learned two things: I was accountable to tell the
truth, and I learned that I was not in the same class as most of the other
children. My family was blue collar, not white collar.

76

Earth School starts when you are born. Being on the path is exactly like being in first grade. How you take the lesson makes all the difference in the world. If you use the lesson for self-deprecation, by turning it against yourself, you will grow a shameful self. If you take the lesson and become angry or frustrated with it, and turn it against others, you will grow a blameful self. Shame and blame are useless. You cannot progress if you indulge in either of these. Knowing this is the key that opens the door to inner freedom. Those two lessons immediately gave me an understanding of life that I did not previously have.

Even though I felt humiliation, I transformed this lesson into honesty and into the acceptance of who *I* am, by not trying to be like all the others. All of the outer circumstances of life that create the tests, challenges and trials, have only one real function: to grow and strengthen our consciousness. If these lessons are *not* rejected or resisted, a great well of perseverance and wisdom is born. A hunger and thirst for greater consciousness is inspired. Stand steady and open, in both your successes and failures. Learn how to take everything and turn it into your benefit. Let the lessons become the strands that you weave into the strong and beautiful fabrics of velvet and wool. Learn how to become an alchemist and turn lead into gold.

Turning Lead Into Gold

You face the mundane, ordinary challenges of life every day. Everyone has his or her own trials. It might be getting through the frenzy of the work day, communicating with others, fulfilling family responsibilities, paying the bills, or preparing meals. Superimposed upon the mundane, there may be even greater challenges such as sickness, divorce, or loss of loved ones.

How do you cultivate acceptance and an open heart when it is hard enough just to get through a day without tension and judgment? The difference between facing those places with peace instead of frustration, with joy instead of boredom, with interest instead of indifference, and with optimism instead of pessimism is by allowing the fire of spiritual practice, commitment, and consciousness to permeate every circumstance we encounter from morning until night, day after day.

The decision to do this is one of the most profound choices you can ever make in your life. From that moment on, you begin to burn through resistance, suppression, and karma. Every encounter and interaction becomes the fuel for deeper spiritual awareness. Every moment holds the potential for clear insight and pure awareness.

Tapas, one of the advanced inner practices of yoga, is the cultivation of enthusiasm and zeal for the spiritual path. It is the willingness to do whatever is necessary to reach a goal with discipline; it is the determination to undertake *sadhana,* daily practice, which burns through the unconscious activity of karma. If this unconscious activity is burned through, instead of being either expressed or repressed in harmful or negative ways, the energetic process of catharsis and release begins. This is the door to transformation and conscious awareness.

Before this choice is made, you may face challenges with resistance, negativity, martyrdom, victimization, or at the very least, disdain. Because it requires you to take responsibility for yourself and for everything in your life, this choice is momentous. When you do not take responsibility, you hold your reactions inside, allowing an internal struggle to set up camp in your body and mind. Your mind engages in ongoing chatter as you defend or justify your thoughts and project them onto a situation or person. Each thought is designed to entrench you in righteousness concerning your own feelings.

While the mind is busily engaged in terrorizing you as well as others, the body is also under attack. The intensity of reaction can result in muscle tension, stomach ache, a tight chest, or a lump in the throat. The longer you engage in suppression, the more serious your physical problems become. Without the ability or the choice to let go into the light of consciousness, you are in the full ravages of suppression. Repeatedly indulging in your reactions to life causes great pain physically, emotionally and spiritually. Yet, most people continue to do this.

That Which We Truly Yearn For

The commitment to spiritual growth, and the decision to bring more conscious awareness into our lives, can purify and transform our reactions into a more subtle response. This allows our energies to continue flowing in our bodies and allows our minds to retain an emptiness or space for awareness without judgment. From the compost of our challenges emerges the fertile soil of awareness, communion, and growth. This is the desire in the deepest part of ourselves that we truly yearn for. We want to see and feel the beauty all around us. We want to shine our lights in joy.

In conscious awareness, we witness or watch everything. We witness our emotions rolling through the body. We witness our thoughts streaming through the mind. From the place of witness, we experience everything while practicing becoming nothing. When there is no holding of an emotion or thought, it is free to flow through. Paradoxically, we see and feel everything, but we hold nothing.

Through this ever deepening practice of allowing life to move through us, all of the past holdings start to melt and release, making room for awareness to meet every moment more fully.

Peace and serenity result from a willingness to engage in surrender—surrender to the situation, surrender to the thoughts and feelings, surrender to the moment. *Ishvara Pranidhana*, is a yogic practice of surrender and service to God. It is the practice of allowing spirit to do its will through us. We can practice this by surrendering to the situation, surrendering to the thoughts and feelings, and surrendering to the moment. While we may be feeling the charge of reaction and anger inside, we can simultaneously allow ourselves to witness and release. This practice becomes the fire which burns through our suppressions and holdings and purifies our being with its heat. This is the fire of *tapas*.

With commitment and practice, you grow the seeds of allowance, acceptance, and peace within your heart and mind. Knowing everyday trials are the fuel for transformation can spark the willingness to accept, look forward to, and even be thankful for every single moment of every single day.

An old story tells of a spiritual seeker who had been meditating in seclusion in the mountains for 20 years. When at last he felt he had achieved his goal of liberation, he set out to return to the village to see his teacher. On his way down the mountain, the seeker met a woman on the path. "Can you give me some water," he asked. "I am very thirsty."

"Find your own—I have barely enough for myself!" she snapped. Filled with indignation and rage, the seeker slapped her across the face. Later, when he had arrived in the village and had found his teacher, he spoke with great remorse. "I must return to the seclusion of meditation, for I still carry the seeds of anger within me." To this his teacher replied, "No, you cannot return. Now you must stay and learn how to find peace in your heart when you are in the world with other people." Like the seeker, we must first integrate our spiritual principles into our daily lives before we can become truly free.

The Lesson is About You

In your own way and at your own pace, you are walking on the path of love. This means you have a call to grow, expand and to be a beautiful person, a good person. How do you succeed at this and how do you fail? On the path, we look at our failures in order to learn from them. We are happy to do this and observe ourselves with great love and compassion.

What happens when you are going forward, and then you start to slip? Maybe you catch yourself through self-reflection. Maybe you do not catch yourself, and fall. What happens in that process?

> *It happened to me a lot this week. My neighbor was angry with me, and I got angry with him. Then I got into an argument with somebody at work.*

What generated that? What caused you to fight and to perpetrate harm through your fight?

> *I felt I was right and he was a jerk; somehow I felt justified.*

The moment you think you are right about something, you are on the wrong track. This is the perfect karmic set-up for you to learn the lesson your soul is trying to learn. The universe is working in harmony for you. Everybody feels justified in their anger; they feel right about what they are saying and feeling. When we are conscious, we go beyond that; we know we are not justified because we are no longer in the right-and-wrong, power-struggle place. So what generates failure, what causes you to fail?

> *The repetition of our karmic pattern?*

Everybody is born with a karmic blueprint. When you leave this plane, you will not be the same as when you came in, because in this continuum called life, you are learning. Every soul learns something. Your blueprint at the end of your life is different from your blueprint at the beginning. You will start your next cycle wherever you leave off. The period between birth and death is really important. It is your learning time when you get to transform the blueprint of your karmic body, or *kayakamma*.

Kamma is a process, action, energy or force. It is our own doings reacting on ourselves. The pain or happiness we experience are the result of our own thoughts, words, and deeds reacting on themselves. Our thoughts, words and deeds produce our prosperity and failure, our happiness and misery.

Karma is released when you learn how not to respond in the same way to the same situation. Your primary pattern created your karma in the past. You were born with that blueprint, and then every experience you have, with whomever you are having it with, is generated by your primary pattern.

When you were young, you learned the rules about how to treat others: *Do this and don't do that.* You thought you understood those rules, but then you found out that you *do* perpetrate harm, and you *do* offend others. You must go beyond that recognition and find out what generates your behavior in order to find your freedom from repetitive actions that cause you pain. You must hold your intention for release by recognizing what you do that keeps you feeling restricted. In order to be free, you have to be willing to look at how you fail yourself. This is what self-reflection and healing are all about, and this is why we give great thanks for the reflections that are teaching us.

Is the pattern different for everyone?

There are variations on a theme. We human beings are all similar in our vibrational, human constitution. The patterns create open holes within us that cannot contain the light. It is like a leak in the plumbing system that cannot contain water. The water comes in but leaks out of the hole and is lost. Most people have these holes within them, and lose their light and love when they repeat the unhealthy patterns.

Begin to identify the ways in which you lose your love. When you feel isolated, separated, burned out, angry, jealous, or needy, you are feeding the hole. When you feel justified in these emotions, you make the hole larger.

You feed the pattern by believing in it. When you stop believing in it, it begins to get cauterized with light. The strands of light weave the fabric of your consciousness back into wholeness so you are no longer losing your light and love. You begin to be able to contain the light consistently and to lift yourself up and be able to serve.

To serve the universe and everything in it, is the great blessing we are born with. If your light is being drained, you cannot serve. Most of the time, you can only take care of yourself because you are losing energy. What do you have left to give if you are losing your light and love down a hole? Identify, through self-reflection, the ways in which you leave yourself and lose your love so you can learn how to contain the light.

Our beliefs about sin are different from those in some other traditions and religions. We sin when we get lost in our unconsciousness and perpetrate harm. We are learning, and we learn through our flaws and failures. We are willing to have the courage to see our failures and to step up and carry on.

It is a powerful time on the planet. What a charge and opportunity we have to serve ourselves and everyone in this place! It is important for you to know how to grow your love in a good way. As you contain the light, you become the light which is infinite.

When you see you are not holding the light, do not skip a beat. With consciousness, lift yourself up into the frequency that is one you choose to resonate with. You can change your resonance by sitting in meditation and focusing awareness on the sound of the breath. Spend time in resonance movement,[4] coordinating body movements with inhaling and exhaling the breath, or by repetition of prayer or mantra. You might also use the connection of the natural, elemental world to lift yourself up by going for a long, silent walk in the forest. These practices help you to remember instantly. This is healing.

As you learn to love yourself deeply and hold light, you will be able to understand other people. *As within, so without.* How can you have understanding for other people if you do not have understanding for yourself first? You cannot. If you have a hole of anger in you, you are going to find all the people who have the same hole, and they are going to reflect it back to you. Give thanks for the people who are helping to show you what you need to see. This is how it works.

Spiritual Attunement in Daily Practice

Bring conscious awareness to your daily *sadhana*, your spiritual practice. Open the sacred energies with the embodiment of gratitude, humility, and respect. Attune to the world of spirit and vibration. How does one attune to spirit? Do so by refining your own frequency or vibration so you resonate with the vibration of love.

The inner journey is energetic. *You* have to make that journey. The frequency is there. To attune your vibration to the subtle frequencies of the inner realms, quiet yourself with the breath and still your body,

---

4   See Resonance Movement, Appendix.

mind, and emotions. Create sacred space and time to be quiet, meditate and pray. This assures your ability to resonate with the frequency of healing and love.

Spiritual attunement in the morning sets the course for the entire day. Upon awakening, prepare yourself briefly: wash your face, brush your teeth, comb your hair, and then go to your place of meditation and sit quietly. Attuning at the beginning of the day, as the energies are rising, is very powerful. If you skip this because you are in a hurry or because you think you will do it later, you will be attuning your frequency to who-knows-what—to the first experience, situation or person you meet. Then, when you enter a stressful workplace, you will vibrate with stress. Or, if you go to the bank and speak with a clerk or a stranger, you will vibrate at that person's frequency. *It is subtle, but it is real.* You have the power to learn discrimination and to choose what you want to vibrate with. Give yourself the opportunity to choose the resonance of love. Remember what you are doing when you are attuning. Remembering will create the difference between an empty ritual and an ecstatic, fulfilling connection. Empty ritual leaves you wondering why nothing has changed. To make your connection, you must change both your physical and energetic chemistry.

Attunement to this resonance allows you to vibrate at the level of the masters. From this place, everything changes. You succeed in being in this world, but not of it. You succeed in being a human being with all of the traits of a human being, and yet you can encounter anything and still vibrate at the point of peace with perfect love and perfect trust. Perfect love and perfect trust are the embodiment of simplicity, clarity and honesty.

Spiritual Alchemy

Alchemy is the physical transformation of lead into gold. On a physical level, we have the ability to bind one substance to another to create a whole new substance. This physical alchemy is a reflection of the vaster and more expansive spiritual possibilities that are created through transformation of the soul.

We take what is heavy— fear, anger, and self-pity—and transform it into self-awareness and finally into love. Prayer, meditation, repetition of mantra, sacred movement, and the breath are powerful tools of consciousness. They are capable of taking us to a frequency that creates healing and light. The breath is the doorway that takes us to the domain of the higher realms of consciousness. When we experience heaviness, we can return to the power of the breath. This creates a space of calm, meditative awareness that enables us to witness the destructive capacity of our some of our feelings. We enter the Assemblage Point of Light[5] and perceive ourselves without judgment, without justification and without analysis.

In spiritual alchemy, our shadow self binds with our divine light, and our profane self binds with our spiritual self. The energy of this binding releases healing and light that frees us from our destructive energies. Fear, anger, and self-pity are truly destructive, relentlessly spinning us in circles. Over and over, they steer us away from spirit. When we meet them with the breath and the Assemblage Point of Light, we transform them and create a new substance. It is like four-wheel drive where the energy of the front and back wheels create far greater power together than either set of wheels can do alone. The meeting of shadow and light, of the profane and the spiritual, transforms our belief that fear, anger, and self-pity are real. In this way, the forces of destruction become our allies, moving us from the unreal to the real, from darkness to light, and from lead to love.

---

[5] See Assemblage Point of Light, Appendix.

Prana dissolves all obstructions effortlessly. The indwelling spiritual intelligence, embodied within the currents of prana, knows how to adjust all variables of physiology, emotion, and thought currents. The simple act of breathing in consciously and breathing out consciously, is the great balancer, the great sustainer, and the great provider. There are no exceptions to this. Prana, the infinite energy of light, is accessed through each breath we take.

Breathing consciously is like tuning in to a relaxing channel of flow and effortlessness, easily dissolving hardness and tension.

Breathe in and listen to the sound and feel the sensation of the long inhalation.

Breathe out and soften, soften, soften . . . .

You cannot change your consciousness without changing your chemistry. Breathe consciously. It will change your chemistry and therefore, your consciousness.

11

ALIGNING WITH SPIRIT

The Great Mystery Guides Us Everyday

When we awaken in the morning, we make a to-do list and immediately fill ourselves with ideas, worries, concerns, frustrations, and angers. We fill ourselves up with the part of ourselves that we strive to let go of on a spiritual path. We strive to let go of the small, childish mind within us and the emotional terrors that plague us. We strive to be peaceful and harmonious, but we wake up in the morning and fill ourselves up with ourselves. When we do that, we falter. We want the great mystery to take us, to be with us and to fill us, but we miss the signs and the grace, we miss everything. We miss the breath and therefore we miss the love. We are so busy in our own small consciousness, plotting, planning, complaining, devising, manipulating, and worrying.

With all the things we do, we miss the great mystery. We miss how amazing it is to be able to breathe in and to breathe out. *I breathe in and I know I'm alive; I breathe out and I give thanks for my life.* Thich Nhat Hanh spoke that prayer, and it is one of the most beautiful prayers I have ever worked with—such a beautiful, simple prayer!

We are alive and we are taken by the great mystery every single day. We do not know we are taken because we hide the great mystery behind our own agenda. We miss what is sacred. The great mystery is always holding us. We miss it, not because it does not come to us, and not because it is not there. It is always there. The eternal love of the mystery is perpetual. We miss it because we are filled with something else at the moment.

Reflect on your contract with God. What is your contract? What is your purpose? What is the point of your day today? What is the point of your life this week? Reflect on your path so you can be living a good life, and fulfilling, for your own soul, the promises you have made to yourself. This is between you and God.

I know what my point is. I uphold the absolute in every moment. What is the absolute? For me the absolute is the consciousness of God. What is the consciousness of God? The consciousness of God is Love. So I strive—I do not always succeed—but I strive every day to uphold the absolute and to be harmonious.

Despite how we think it goes, the Great Mystery is in charge. We make assumptions, judgments and draw conclusions, and then everything we thought we knew changes. What do we know? We do not know anything, so we strive to be able to trust love. What is love? What is trusting love? Trusting love is allowing the great mystery to guide us.

Flowing with Surrender

In the morning I become quiet. I listen with my feeling center so I can know what to do and how to do it. It does not matter what laundry list has accumulated, made up of the many things that need to be taken care of. I have that list, but I use it only as a kind of light frame of reference because every day something happens that I did not know was going to happen, and I need to shift.

I made peace a long time ago with living in a state of surrender so that I am very comfortable with shifting things when spirit tells me to do so. When something comes up that is difficult to shift, I shift it. If I need to change an appointment or call someone and say, "I'm sorry, this isn't going to work for me right now, let's see if we can change this,"

I am very comfortable. I am comfortable if I say, "Yes I will," and then Spirit says a little bit later, "No, you won't." I am very honest and I say, "I thought I could, but I cannot and I'm so sorry." And I am sincere in what I say.

In a surrendered state, you cannot care what people think about you, you cannot think highly of yourself, and you cannot get attached to what you want. When you live a surrendered life, you live with risk, you live with saying or doing things that might be uncomfortable to say or do.

When I was a young woman, I was standing on a road in a deeply wooded part of New Hampshire, and as I looked into the woods, I knew there was going to be a healing center there. I knew it with every fiber of my being. I had no idea how it could happen because I had just finished building a house, with no mortgage, with my own hands. To even *think* of building a healing center seemed crazy. Later, I also felt strongly inspired to travel to Cape Breton. Once I was on the island, I knew that I was going to build a Sanctuary there. Both of these things came to pass, and much more, as a result of my willingness to go with the flow of spirit.

When I look back at the tasks before me then, there was no way I could have said, on an impulse, "Sure, let's do that." Without the flow of spirit within me, around me, behind me and all about me, I could not have done these things on my own. Opening to this ebb and flow and allowing yourself to surrender to what spirit wants for you to fulfill the divine plan, holds a tremendous amount of synchronicity, accomplishment and joy. The divine plan does not necessarily mean you have to move to Calcutta and become a nun; it might, but it also means how we live our ordinary lives, each and every moment, each and every day.

The art of surrendering is extraordinarily beautiful, and that is when Spirit can use you. When Spirit cannot use you, you get stuck in between, in a kind of Purgatory. There is a Purgatory, and it is neither here nor there, it is neither up nor down, it is neither heaven nor hell. When you do not live a surrendered life, you live a life in Purgatory. You are not doing anything. You are going on automatic pilot day by day. It is not hell, it is not heaven, it is just somewhere in between that is void of light.

When you condition yourself to the ebb and flow of Spirit, all ego resistance that says, "This is too risky," is gone. It disappears. Your resistance is just a trap to keep you comfortable and immobile, and most of all to keep you from doing any good in the world.

I cannot help but feel things, but I don't always move quickly on what I feel.

You do not move quickly because you go into your head. It comes to you, but then you hesitate or talk yourself out of it, which is very common. Perhaps you are drawn sideways by what other people are thinking, by your own fears, or even by your reluctance to make a commitment. Or, you may not want to diverge from the beliefs and norms of the collective. When you very clearly feel the light of Spirit, your experience is vertical. You have to train yourself to activate that direct, vertical line to bring yourself into ascension. Learn how to open the channel and quickly align, not with someone or something else, but directly with Spirit.

Focusing the Mind

Reflect on how you go through your day. What do you do? Watch all the ways in which your mind wanders. Watch how it takes you away from your meditative awareness and causes you to lose focus. When your unruly mind pulls you around, you become watered down. You cannot live in a surrendered state unless you learn to focus your higher mind on the task at hand, which is the one that is given you by God. What does focus mean? Focus means that your mind is under control so that you can follow the *prana,* or the surrendered flow of Spirit. When Spirit gives you something to do, you are focused on getting it done.

The way we live life can be a meditation, a meditation in motion. When you are distracted, thinking about politics or about the cruise two months down the road, you are no longer meditating. Meditation is stilling and focusing the mind. You do not just do it when you are sitting; one can meditate all the time. Focus on whatever task is at hand. *But, what about this task over here?* Well, when this is done, you will get to that. Without focus, the energy gets dissipated and watered down. It gets disassembled, and then you get overwhelmed, and you do not feel like doing any of it. You are sunk before you have even succeeded in focusing on one, just *one,* place that you have been given to focus upon.

Spiritual Practice is Lifelong

Change your karma by doing spiritual practice: meditation, prayer, sacred movement, and engaging the witness consciousness. Watch yourself from your higher Self so that you do not go on automatic. When you feel yourself wanting to react in the same old way, breathe. The breath gives you a moment to bring in a completely different energy rather than the relentless, repetitious reaction that you regularly have. The breath allows you to go into witness consciousness and to take a moment to redirect the habitual, unconscious patterns of what it is that you perpetually say, think or do. One long breath in, and one long breath out, will change everything. Focus on nothing except the sound and sensation of the breath. Know the breath is the tool you are using, in this moment of consciousness, to transform yourself.

We go through this same process day after day, year after year. It is the lifelong ebb and flow of following Spirit, and that is how we transform ourselves. There is nothing new or esoteric about any of this; it is the simple, transformative, contemplative practice that we apply every day, all day long, to the best of our ability.

We also give ourselves concentrated retreat time to help us anchor what it feels like to be spending more time in meditation, chanting, an in self-reflection. In deeper retreat time, we can feel the difference. We desire to bring that experience into our everyday lives so we are never away from it. That desire is the desire to be melded with the absolute.

Conscious awareness brings you to your real self. You do not have to think about what to do. You do not have to process it, it is just there. Use your spiritual tools to change and transform your consciousness.

As a result of transformation, you will not have to go into your head to muddle and spin, and you will not react out of an individual, karmic place. You are no longer stuck in the karmic groove; you are free.

When I breathe, I can feel everything expand. Is that because the breath brings us to God?

The breath *is* God. The breath is *prana*, and *prana* is the energy and consciousness of God. Without breath, there is no life. We have to breathe. Almost everybody breathes unconsciously all day long. If you are alive and walking around, you are breathing. But breathing consciously is a different matter. Breathing consciously allows you to change your consciousness. So when you are breathing in the breath, it is the breath of God, the *prana* of universal intelligence.

With practice, the breath can feel expansive and relaxing. It can change your consciousness in a moment, transforming the places that plague you: worries, fears, frustrations, insecurities and angers. You can change your consciousness by focusing on the breath for just a few minutes. It is the breath of God, it is prana, it is the golden life force.

Of all the spiritual practices, the breath is the most powerful. The breath is the great transformer. In the beginning it may feel awkward and a little mechanical, but if you stay with the breath long enough, you start to dissolve these places. You begin to soften. When you exhale, let go and relax. When you inhale, fill yourself up and rejuvenate. Five minutes of *pranayama*, of breathing consciously, can be more powerful than an hour of yoga. It is good to remember to breathe.

In the morning, instead of saying to my husband, "Have a nice day, honey," I say, "Remember to breathe." During the work day, the breath helps you to field all of the stress and brings your awareness back to the present moment and into balance. When you are going too fast, the breath will slow you down, and when you are going too slow, it will lift you up. It makes the perfect adjustment without your having to know what the intelligence of the *prana* is doing. The *prana* is divine intelligence. It regulates us without our having to do anything except the most natural thing in the world, which is to breathe. It is the first thing we do when we are born. When we are born, we breathe in and it is an inhale, and when we die, we breathe out and it is an exhale. Our life is one long breath.

I encourage you to not be comfortable. I encourage you to not do everything the same way all of the time. I encourage you to give more, I encourage you to open more, I encourage you to feel more. I encourage you to embody a true beginner's mind, realizing that you know nothing about anything. And therefore, infinite possibilities are available to you from the infinite source of abundance and love. As your mind is empty and you know that you know nothing, all is given because there is space for it to be received. True humility is your best friend. As you go deep, shed your self-image, shed your preferences, shed your opinions, shed your likes and your dislikes. Be fluid in the stream of love.

CHAPTER

12

EQUALIZE HAPPINESS AND SORROW

In the beginning of the *Bhagavad Gita*, the warrior-Prince, Arjuna, seeks counsel on the battlefield from his charioteer, Lord Krishna. Arjuna is overcome with tears because his efforts for leading a life that brings fulfillment have not been realized, and he is pleading for help and guidance. Krishna explains that our greatest battles are within our own minds. Among his words to Arjuna are these: *By even-mindedness equalize happiness and sorrow, profit and loss, triumph and failure — so encounter the battle! Thus thou wilt not acquire sin.*[6]

How does the earnest student stabilize the currents of mind and achieve the mental equilibrium described by Krishna? Mental equilibrium diminishes our investment in belief systems, past conditioning, and desires for the future. It is a result of living in pure witness where there is no investment in position or opinion. Consider for a moment being so present and neutral that you are no longer influenced by the repetitive, corrosive action of the perpetual, unconscious response that is karma. Consider developing a neutral response which does not include investing in the polarities of to do or not to do, to want or not to want, to have or not to have, and so on.

---

[6]   Verse 38 in *God Talks with Arjuna: The Bhagavad Gita* by Paramahansa Yogananda. 1995: Self-Realization Fellowship.

In witness consciousness, the events, challenges, and scenes of life become like a cosmic dream. If you are not emotionally invested in this dream, then it loses its significance. It especially loses its hurtful effects and frees the heart and soul to meet the present moment without resistance, judgment or censorship. It not only releases the hurtful responses, but it also releases the potential to be swayed by preferences, attachments, addictions or obsessions. The spiritual adept embodies even-mindedness while enacting his or her part in the cosmic dream, even while the clash of opposites is playing out.

Great empowerment is realized by becoming strong in the core of one's being. What may appear to be aloofness or going on automatic pilot in the adept is actually mastery over contrary emotions created by attachments and longings. So for a moment, consider no opinion, no position. What are your preferences? What are your attachments? What are your addictions? What are your obsessions? To dwell peacefully in no opinion and no position, one must be a persistent seeker who has already experienced enough despondency in life to sincerely ask for help.

Arjuna's frustration and sorrow are the goads for his spiritual progress. The nature of the soul is to progress toward spirit. If the soul did not have this desire for spiritual progress, no discouragement or regret would ever be felt. The first chapter of the *Gita* is referred to as "Arjuna Vishada Yoga," which loosely translated means, *the sorrow the seeker feels that first creates a longing for unification with God.*

When the soul is tested and one has experienced enough discouragement, a possibility exists for spirit to enter. A chink in the armor of ego lets in a ray of light for the option to self-reflect on one's obsessions. When obsessions are released, the soul can then self-reflect on one's addictions. When addictions are released, the soul can then self-reflect on one's attachments. When attachments are released, the soul can then self-reflect on one's preferences. When preferences are released, the soul can then experience no opinion and no position. It is here that the calmness of spiritual surrender and the purity of witness consciousness, in union with receptive devotion, can permeate the consciousness of the individual soul essence. It is here that the release of personal desires, expectations and delusions gives way to the voice of spirit within and intuitive awareness unfolds into a river of union between the individual and God. This establishes the consciousness of the true self.

APPENDIX

1: *The Golden Circle Breath*

The breath is the entry point to deeper levels of consciousness. The breath awakens prana in the physical body and the light body. There is a deep relationship between breath, thought, emotions, and movement. They interact with and affect each other. Breath acts as a link between the physical, mental, and emotional bodies. The breath is used as a powerful tool to gather the scattered forces of all the bodies to function harmoniously in integration. The breath heals the underlying conflict that exists between what you are thinking, feeling, and doing. This conflict is the source of all persistent conditions that manifest on the physical, mental and emotional levels. The combination of the breath with consciousness creates a harmonizing effect upon the unconscious forces that keep you from being healthy and relaxed.

The golden circle breath can be done in an upright, seated position, with the spine erect, or can be done lying down. Inhale through the nose, drawing the breath in slowly. Contract the back of the throat slightly and draw the breath in making an "ahhhhh" sound. The mouth remains closed. As the air passes over the windpipe it sounds like air inflating a tire. By contracting the back of the throat, the air flow can be regulated, thereby allowing the inhalation and exhalation to be prolonged. Continue with long, slow inhalations. Let the abdomen relax and expand as you inhale and receive the breath.

Exhale slowly as you pull the abdomen in and up to fully empty your lungs. Control the flow of the breath. Naturally and gradually, as you relax into the breath, the breath will start to "breathe itself". Now, begin to visualize breathing in golden light. Starting at the perineum, as you inhale, bring the golden light slowly up to the crown. As you exhale, complete the circle by breathing the golden light down the back, returning to the base of the spine.

Continue to breath a strong, steady inhale of golden light, from the base of the spine, up to the crown, exhaling, complete the golden circle back down from the crown, returning to the base of the spine. This creates a full circle of golden light. Expand this light until you are sitting in the middle of a radiant orb of golden light. Gently bring your hands into the golden seal and dissolve into the golden circle breath.

The Golden Seal

The Golden Seal is a simple hand position. The right hand is held by the left hand. The hands remain relaxed. The right fingers sit gently upon the left fingers, the left thumb sits on the right thumbnail. You can see through the cracks of your fingers. The hands can be held low or up higher up, wherever is comfortable and natural, depending of the length of your arms. This seal completes the energetic circuitry in your physical and energy body to hold and sustain the golden light. You can use this seal in the practice of meditation.

2: The Assemblage Point of Light

The golden circle breath creates an infusion of healing, golden light. As we become adept at sustaining this golden light, through regular practice, we can, simply by closing our eyes and consciously returning to the golden circle breath, access this light quickly and easily. The golden circle breath contains within it, the absolute. This absolute energy is self-existing, self-fulfilling and self-sustaining. It is an ever-constant source of energy, which stabilizes the ever-shifting currents of life.

Returning, again and again, to the assemblage point of light, allows us to withstand the cycles of disassembly and assembly. Because we are shifting constantly and at a more rapid pace than ever, the threat of destabilization through disassembly is probable. These cycles are not going to go away. These cycles will, in fact, accelerate even more.

As you breathe, and sustain the light within you, you become an agent for stabilizing these erratic energies and cycles, not only for yourself but for everyone. You will not get stuck, overwhelmed or afraid, if you make a conscious choice to be in this light. Through the golden circle breath, you return to the assemblage point of light. It is an infinite, strong and healing source, which you can return to and rely on.

The assemblage point of light is pure. It is neutral. It does not judge. It observes everything, from a completely neutral vantage point. From this point of light, you can sustain and stabilize great challenges, which are the result of shifting into the new paradigm of consciousness. Your ability to hold and sustain this light within you is your ability to know, and exist with God. The assemblage point of light is the point from which our higher consciousness observes the emotional life of the self. We see ourselves from a neutral, detached position, without judgment, analysis, embarrassment, doubt or fear. We regard ourselves without an impulse to alter our circumstances or ourselves. From this place, we can experience the darkest night of feeling as we watch ourselves calmly and with clarity. The non-attachment of the assemblage point of light is not one of disassociation from feeling, but rather the courage to enter into feeling with open eyes. From here we recognize our feeling without any need to think it into self-justification, self-pity, or self-criticism. Our most challenging feelings then, remain unattached from our identity. Our thoughts have not influenced our insecurity, fear, anger or our sadness, into a sense of who we are.

We enter this light by the action of the breath and we can enter it at any time. At work, in relationships, at play, in a traffic jam, we can breathe ourselves into the assemblage point of light. By consciously breathing the slow, steady and continuous golden circle breath, we can suddenly move from unconsciousness to higher consciousness. From this place you will know yourself better and spiritually refine who you are. You will neutrally watch your feelings pass through like clouds moving through the sky, you will feel their energy, without engaging that energy. This practice allows you to recognize them quickly, and release them easily. You learn how to let go. This is an entry point into higher consciousness. When you bring yourself to The assemblage point of light often, you create your own healing.

This is what love is, the acceptance of the self. The heart knows the spirit and it expands within the light of higher consciousness. The assemblage point of light exists in the dialogue between the heart and third eye. The heart opens to accept the self and one's higher consciousness sheds light upon the heart.

The assemblage point of light is realized both in the physical body, and the energy body. In the physical body it is realized through the heart charka. In the energy body, it is realized through the third eye. It is contained within the golden circle breath. As you breath, you become powerful – full of light and full of the power of love. Breathe in and know you are alive. Breathe out and know you are love.

3: *The Resonance of the Stillpoint*

When the golden infusion of light, which is the result of the golden circle breath and the golden seal, assembles around, and in your body, (the assemblage point of Light), the phenomena of the resonance of the stillpoint can be realized, a deep concentrative state of meditation. Healing is a resonance. Resonance is a state in which a vibration or frequency is produced, in response to an external stimulus, occurring when the frequency of the stimulus is the same. If you have two violins, tuned the same, and on one violin a sound is produced by vibrating one chord, the other violin will start to vibrate the same chord. The violin which was resonating, through sound, at a higher frequency, stimulated the silent violin to be able to resonate from a lower frequency, (no sound), to a higher frequency (sound).

This universal law of resonance is not only true in relationship to the physical dimension, through the laws of physics, but also to the spiritual dimensions, through the universal laws of metaphysics.

Cosmic intelligence, or consciousness, is held within the oscillating frequency of the breath. This cosmic intelligence is light and resonates at an extremely high frequency. It is the frequency of the One, or, energy, which exists at an undivided level. Because it is undivided, undifferentiated energy, it is whole and unified. Healing of the body, heart, mind and spirit occurs in this whole energy. Therefore, healing is a resonance. Healing can occur as the higher frequency stimulates the lower frequency up to its' level. This is why a group of people who meditate and pray together can successfully have a positive influence in the place they are meditating, or on the persons they are praying for. A synchronization of frequency, through group spiritual practices, can exponentially amplify this frequency and create a positive effect, which may otherwise, not have been able to be realized by an individual.

Likewise, even one individual who has realized how to sustain higher levels of consciousness, or higher levels of resonance, can positively affect many other individuals. The more stable the resonance, the more positive the effect.

Simplicity and realization is at the heart of all understanding. It is very simple to consciously breathe in and out. It is simple to visualize the radiance of the Golden Light around you, as you breathe. It is so simple, that most people cannot grasp that this simple practice can lead you to God. Or, that meditating or praying with others can, potentially, heal everyone.

Close your eyes, drawing your attention inward. Take some deep relaxing breaths. Soften any holding in your face, shoulders, belly, legs. Slowly and naturally, begin the golden circle breath and place your hands in the golden seal position. Take time here to deeply relax and align with the healing power of the breath. Allow the Light to start to infuse you as you visualize a beautiful golden orb, which is both in and around you. This is the assemblage point of light. Continue to allow yourself to deepen into the breath. Bring your awareness to your heart, throat and third eye. Absorb the light.

Surrender to the resonance of this golden light. Soften into its energy. Experience the wholeness of this resonance. Become the resonance of the stillpoint as you completely blend with this golden light. Become powerful – full of light and full of the power of love. Breathe in and know you are alive. Breathe out and know you are love.

4: Resonance Movement

Resonance Movement is a contemplative practice that coordinates conscious breath with conscious movement. When the breath and movement are unified, the consciousness of the body, heart, mind and spirit enters a state of deep relaxation and healing. The breathing technique is both powerful and simple. The body movements are gentle and flowing, yet strengthening and intense.

Through the golden circle breath, energy is intensified in and around the body. The nature of the breath is round. The movements create arcs through the arm and body positions which act as a container for this energy. The nature of the movements is round. As you flow through the movements, the energy of golden light builds and intensifies while a slow, relaxing and deepening release of tensions occurs. Transformation happens. Your consciousness reaches new and deeper levels of subtle awareness. Healing occurs on all levels.

Resonance Movement begins with a series of slow-motion passes. Each of these passes is created through the coordination of the golden circle breath with arm movements that are gracefully arced while in various stages of movement. During this phase of Resonance Movement, energies are becoming activated. The golden light, which is the essence of this vital energy, steadily shines and increasingly brightens. This is the assemblage point of light. The body warms up and relaxes. Circulation increases making the body ready for the series of movements. These passes are the foundation for the remaining sequence of movements. They open the door to the breath, coordinate the breath with the body, and create a container to hold the Golden Light.

The sequence of movements, with the breath, deepens your experience of the resonance of the stillpoint. The stillpoint is peaceful. It is openly relaxed. It is softly strong. It is subtly profound. The resonance of the stillpoint is a state of deep meditation. It is the attunement to love. Resonance Movement can be practiced by anyone, at any age, at any level of development. All that is needed, is a desire to become more peaceful, harmonious, and healthy.

Resonance Movement is an intuitive emergence and evolution of contemplative practice. I practiced classical yoga and meditation for over 30 years. Yoga postures are traditionally defined by "lines and extensions of energy in the body." Resonance Movement is realized as "arcs of circular energy and light which exist within the breath and are contained and sustained within the movements."

Resonance Movement is a perfect practice to create harmony in these times. A high degree of light is required to burn up the pressures, stresses, and challenges that affect us from the world we live in. Resonance Movement offers us a way to not only access this universal energy, but a powerful way to sustain it *and* become a container for it. While the effects of Resonance Movement have the power to transform these challenges, its essence is light, soft, and receptive.

5: Communion with the Holy Spirit

Integrative Awareness happens as a result of the breath bringing you into ever deepening levels of consciousness. Each level creates purification of thought and emotion through the sustained practice of daily meditation, developing and stabilizing the witness, engaging in self-observation and inner focus and establishing clear intention. The actualization of meditative awareness manifests as a paradox where opposites happen simultaneously. When the experience of meditation becomes the merging of the body, mind, heart, and soul, the miracle of paradoxical union happens. It is experienced as effortless effort, non-doing in doing, and emptiness in fullness. For your entire being to be the temple of the divine, your practice must harness and harmonize the conflicting forces and disturbances that arise from the body, emotions and mind. These unconscious forces keep you divided and fragmented in your thinking, feeling and doing. The conscious forces of breath, light and stillness create integration and communion with the Holy Spirit.

GLOSSARY

Feeling center - located in the abdominal cavity three finger widths below and two finger widths behind the navel. It corresponds with the physical centre of gravity. The feeling center is a gateway for body energy to pass from one aspect of the body to another such as from the energy body into the physical or from the energy body into spirit. Becoming aware of the feeling center allows us to tune into guidance we can receive from the spiritual dimensions.

Energy body - the first layer, closest to the physical body in the human energy field or aura, also referred to as the auric field or light body. It sustains the physical body and also connects with the higher bodies. It is also the vehicle by which prana enters the body.

Vibrational human constitution –Essentially we are beings of light. It is our light that maintains our physical, emotional and spiritual well-being. The human constitution is made up of several layers that extend beyond and around the physical body and are vibrating with various energies.

Prana - is the original life force. It is a universal energy, a metaphysical substance, responsible for the body's life, heat and maintenance and which constantly circulates through the body. The prana within us is a part of the universal prana. You can unite yourself with the universal prana, and can draw the required amount of prana whenever you need.

Pranayama - is the conscious awareness of breath: the life force that both energizes and relaxes the body. The term is derived from the Sanskrit, prana, meaning "life force," and *ayama*, meaning "extension." The controlled breathing enables a relaxing of the mind for meditation. Each stage of pranayama has the effect of enhancing physical awareness and enforcing introspection. The practices of pranayama conduct prana into the body.

Absolute - a state of consciousness that unifies and accepts all manifestation as it is, in the present moment. It does not stand for or against anything. It is a universal, fixed consciousness.

Primary pattern - the chief pattern that expresses itself through unconscious, repetitive behavior.

Sadhana - the discipline of routine spiritual practice and the routine surrendering of the ego through activities such as meditation, yoga, chanting or prayer.

ABOUT THE AUTHOR

A unique combination of mystic, teacher and author, Maresha is the international founder and resident teacher of The Snow Dragon Sanctuary. The Sanctuary is a contemplative center for all faiths and traditions. Maresha has guided and inspired countless students during her 30 year teaching and healing ministry. As a teacher, her special gift is her ability to communicate the deepest wisdom of the ages to modern seekers. She is able to weave esoteric teachings from several traditions into practical methods that anyone can adopt.

As a dedicated practitioner of unity consciousness, she has distilled more than three decades of study, training, and depth of practice and experience into her teachings.

Maresha holds degrees in Teaching, Education and Wholistic and Macrobiotic counseling and energy medicine. She is also a senior Amrit Yoga teacher and an initiate of the Kundalini Shaktipat tradition. She is the founder of Resonance Movement and Resonance Healing.

Her vision to help people harmonize by living in conscious connection to the divine and to create personal health and joy in living is expressed in her teachings and writings.

mareshaducharmebooks.com
snowsdragonsanctuary.com
603-630-1548

Printed in the United States
By Bookmasters